50 Cinnamon Recipes for Home

By: Kelly Johnson

Table of Contents

- Cinnamon Roll Pancakes
- Classic Cinnamon Rolls
- Cinnamon Sugar Donuts
- Cinnamon Apple Muffins
- Cinnamon Swirl Bread
- Cinnamon Streusel Coffee Cake
- Cinnamon Oatmeal Cookies
- Cinnamon French Toast
- Cinnamon Pear Compote
- Cinnamon Raisin Bagels
- Cinnamon Spiced Nuts
- Cinnamon Maple Granola
- Cinnamon Chocolate Chip Scones
- Cinnamon Apple Crumble
- Cinnamon Pumpkin Bread
- Cinnamon Sugar Pretzels
- Cinnamon Cream Cheese Frosting
- Cinnamon Baked Apples
- Cinnamon Sticky Buns
- Cinnamon Roll Waffles
- Cinnamon Coffee Cake Muffins
- Cinnamon Sugar Popcorn
- Cinnamon Swirl Pancakes
- Cinnamon Pecan Sticky Buns
- Cinnamon Ice Cream
- Cinnamon Banana Bread
- Cinnamon Swirl Cheesecake
- Cinnamon-Spiced Sweet Potatoes
- Cinnamon Almond Granola Bars
- Cinnamon Hot Chocolate
- Cinnamon Roll Cheesecake
- Cinnamon Apple Scones
- Cinnamon and Honey Butter
- Cinnamon Flavored Syrup
- Cinnamon Spiced Rice Pudding
- Cinnamon Swirl Cake

- Cinnamon Raisin Overnight Oats
- Cinnamon and Nutmeg Pancakes
- Cinnamon Apple Smoothie
- Cinnamon Caramel Sauce
- Cinnamon Sugar Shortbread Cookies
- Cinnamon Maple Bacon
- Cinnamon Swirled Cupcakes
- Cinnamon-Spiced Pumpkin Muffins
- Cinnamon Orange Bread
- Cinnamon Rice Cakes
- Cinnamon-Spiced Hot Cider
- Cinnamon Banana Smoothie
- Cinnamon Roll Bars
- Cinnamon Apple Stuffed Pancakes

Cinnamon Roll Pancakes

Ingredients:

For the Pancakes:

- 1 1/2 cups all-purpose flour
- 2 tbsp granulated sugar
- 1 tbsp baking powder
- 1/2 tsp salt
- 1 cup milk
- 1 large egg
- 2 tbsp melted butter
- 1 tsp vanilla extract

For the Cinnamon Swirl:

- 1/4 cup granulated sugar
- 1 tbsp ground cinnamon
- 2 tbsp melted butter

For the Cream Cheese Glaze:

- 4 oz cream cheese, softened
- 1/2 cup powdered sugar
- 2 tbsp milk
- 1/2 tsp vanilla extract

Instructions:

1. **Prepare the Cinnamon Swirl:**
   - In a small bowl, mix together the granulated sugar, ground cinnamon, and melted butter until combined. Set aside.
2. **Prepare the Pancake Batter:**
   - In a large bowl, whisk together the flour, granulated sugar, baking powder, and salt.
   - In another bowl, whisk together the milk, egg, melted butter, and vanilla extract.
   - Pour the wet ingredients into the dry ingredients and stir until just combined. The batter will be slightly lumpy, which is okay.
3. **Heat the Griddle or Pan:**
   - Preheat a non-stick griddle or skillet over medium heat. Lightly grease with butter or cooking spray.
4. **Cook the Pancakes:**
   - Pour about 1/4 cup of pancake batter onto the griddle or skillet for each pancake.

- Immediately drizzle some of the cinnamon swirl mixture over the batter in a swirl pattern. Use a toothpick or the tip of a knife to gently swirl the cinnamon mixture into the pancake batter.
- Cook until bubbles form on the surface and the edges look set, about 2-3 minutes. Flip the pancake and cook for another 1-2 minutes, until golden brown and cooked through.
- Repeat with the remaining batter and cinnamon swirl mixture.

5. **Prepare the Cream Cheese Glaze:**
    - In a medium bowl, beat the softened cream cheese with an electric mixer until smooth.
    - Gradually add the powdered sugar, beating until combined.
    - Add the milk and vanilla extract, and continue to beat until the glaze reaches a smooth and pourable consistency.

6. **Serve:**
    - Stack the pancakes on plates and drizzle with the cream cheese glaze.
    - Serve warm, and enjoy with additional toppings if desired, such as fresh berries, syrup, or extra cinnamon sugar.

Tips:

- **Consistency:** If the pancake batter is too thick, you can add a little more milk to reach your desired consistency.
- **Swirl Pattern:** For a more uniform swirl, use a squeeze bottle to apply the cinnamon mixture or simply drizzle it carefully with a spoon.
- **Make-Ahead:** You can prepare the cinnamon swirl and cream cheese glaze ahead of time and store them in the refrigerator. Just reheat the swirl slightly before using and stir the glaze before drizzling.

These Cinnamon Roll Pancakes bring together the best of both worlds with their sweet, cinnamon flavor and fluffy texture. They're perfect for a special breakfast or brunch!

Classic Cinnamon Rolls

Ingredients:

For the Dough:

- 1 cup milk
- 1/4 cup unsalted butter
- 1/4 cup granulated sugar
- 2 1/4 tsp active dry yeast (1 packet)
- 2 large eggs
- 4 cups all-purpose flour
- 1/2 tsp salt

For the Cinnamon Filling:

- 1/2 cup unsalted butter, softened
- 1 cup brown sugar
- 2 tbsp ground cinnamon
- 1/4 tsp ground nutmeg (optional)

For the Cream Cheese Glaze:

- 4 oz cream cheese, softened
- 1/4 cup unsalted butter, softened
- 1 1/2 cups powdered sugar
- 1/2 tsp vanilla extract
- 2-3 tbsp milk (adjust for consistency)

Instructions:

1. **Prepare the Dough:**
   - In a small saucepan, heat the milk and 1/4 cup butter over medium heat until the butter melts and the mixture is warm but not hot (about 110°F or 45°C).
   - Remove from heat and stir in the granulated sugar. Sprinkle the yeast over the milk mixture and let it sit for 5-10 minutes until foamy.
2. **Mix Dough:**
   - In a large mixing bowl, combine 3 1/2 cups of flour and salt. Make a well in the center and pour in the yeast mixture and eggs.
   - Mix until a dough forms. If the dough is too sticky, gradually add the remaining 1/2 cup of flour until the dough is soft and manageable.
3. **Knead and Rise:**
   - Turn the dough out onto a floured surface and knead for about 5-7 minutes until smooth and elastic.
   - Place the dough in a lightly greased bowl, cover with a damp cloth or plastic wrap, and let it rise in a warm place for about 1-2 hours, or until doubled in size.

4. **Prepare the Filling:**
   - In a small bowl, mix together the softened butter, brown sugar, cinnamon, and nutmeg (if using) until smooth.
5. **Roll Out the Dough:**
   - After the dough has risen, punch it down and turn it out onto a floured surface. Roll it out into a 16x12-inch rectangle.
6. **Spread the Filling:**
   - Evenly spread the cinnamon filling over the dough, leaving a small border around the edges.
7. **Roll and Slice:**
   - Starting from the long edge, carefully roll the dough into a tight log. Pinch the seam to seal.
   - Slice the roll into 12 equal pieces and place them in a greased 9x13-inch baking dish or on a parchment-lined baking sheet.
8. **Second Rise:**
   - Cover the rolls with a damp cloth or plastic wrap and let them rise in a warm place for about 30 minutes, or until they have doubled in size.
9. **Bake:**
   - Preheat the oven to 350°F (175°C).
   - Bake the cinnamon rolls for 20-25 minutes, or until golden brown.
10. **Prepare the Glaze:**
    - While the rolls are baking, beat together the cream cheese and butter until smooth.
    - Gradually add the powdered sugar, vanilla extract, and milk, mixing until the glaze reaches a smooth, pourable consistency.
11. **Glaze and Serve:**
    - Remove the cinnamon rolls from the oven and let them cool slightly before glazing.
    - Drizzle the cream cheese glaze over the warm rolls.

Tips:

- **Flour:** The amount of flour needed can vary. Add flour gradually to avoid a dry dough.
- **Rise Time:** If the dough is not rising well, make sure your yeast is fresh and the environment is warm.
- **Overnight Option:** You can prepare the rolls up to the second rise, then cover and refrigerate overnight. In the morning, let them come to room temperature and rise for about 30 minutes before baking.

Enjoy these classic cinnamon rolls fresh out of the oven for a sweet and comforting treat!

Cinnamon Sugar Donuts

Ingredients:

For the Donuts:

- 2 1/4 tsp active dry yeast (1 packet)
- 1/4 cup warm milk (110°F or 45°C)
- 1/4 cup granulated sugar
- 1/4 cup unsalted butter, softened
- 1/2 tsp salt
- 1/2 tsp ground nutmeg (optional)
- 2 large eggs
- 2 cups all-purpose flour (plus more for dusting)

For the Cinnamon Sugar Coating:

- 1/2 cup granulated sugar
- 1 tbsp ground cinnamon
- 1/4 cup unsalted butter, melted

Instructions:

Frying Method:

1. **Prepare the Dough:**
    - In a small bowl, dissolve the yeast in the warm milk and let it sit for about 5-10 minutes until frothy.
    - In a large mixing bowl, combine the sugar, butter, salt, and nutmeg. Add the yeast mixture and eggs, and mix until combined.
    - Gradually add the flour, mixing until a soft dough forms. You may need to add a little more flour if the dough is too sticky.
2. **Knead and Rise:**
    - Turn the dough out onto a floured surface and knead for about 5-7 minutes until smooth.
    - Place the dough in a greased bowl, cover with plastic wrap or a damp cloth, and let it rise in a warm place for about 1 hour, or until doubled in size.
3. **Roll Out and Cut:**
    - Punch down the dough and turn it out onto a floured surface. Roll out to about 1/2-inch thickness.
    - Use a donut cutter or two round cutters to cut out donuts and holes.
4. **Fry the Donuts:**
    - Heat oil in a deep fryer or heavy-bottomed pot to 350°F (175°C). Fry the donuts in batches, being careful not to overcrowd the pot.
    - Fry for about 1-2 minutes per side, or until golden brown. Use a slotted spoon to transfer the donuts to a paper towel-lined plate to drain.

5. **Coat the Donuts:**
   - Mix the granulated sugar and ground cinnamon in a bowl.
   - Brush each donut with melted butter, then coat evenly with the cinnamon sugar mixture.

Baking Method:

1. **Prepare the Dough:**
   - Follow the same steps as for the frying method to prepare and rise the dough.
2. **Roll Out and Cut:**
   - Roll out the dough and cut out the donuts and holes as described above.
3. **Bake the Donuts:**
   - Preheat the oven to 375°F (190°C).
   - Place the donut shapes on a greased or parchment-lined baking sheet.
   - Bake for 8-10 minutes, or until the donuts are golden brown.
4. **Coat the Donuts:**
   - Brush with melted butter and coat with cinnamon sugar as described above.

Tips:

- **Oil Temperature:** For frying, ensure the oil temperature is correct to avoid greasy donuts. Use a candy thermometer to monitor the temperature.
- **Flour:** Be cautious not to add too much flour; the dough should be soft and slightly sticky.
- **Donut Cutter:** If you don't have a donut cutter, use two different-sized round cutters or a large and small glass.

These Cinnamon Sugar Donuts are perfect for breakfast or a sweet treat. Whether you fry or bake them, they're sure to be a hit!

Cinnamon Apple Muffins

Ingredients:

For the Muffins:

- 1 1/2 cups all-purpose flour
- 1/2 cup granulated sugar
- 1/2 cup packed brown sugar
- 1/2 tsp baking soda
- 1 1/2 tsp baking powder
- 1/2 tsp salt
- 1/2 tsp ground cinnamon
- 1/4 tsp ground nutmeg (optional)
- 1/2 cup unsalted butter, melted
- 1/2 cup milk
- 2 large eggs
- 1 tsp vanilla extract
- 1 1/2 cups peeled, cored, and diced apples (about 1-2 apples, such as Granny Smith or Honeycrisp)

For the Cinnamon Sugar Topping:

- 2 tbsp granulated sugar
- 1 tsp ground cinnamon
- 1 tbsp unsalted butter, melted

Instructions:

1. **Prepare the Oven and Pan:**
   - Preheat your oven to 350°F (175°C). Line a 12-cup muffin tin with paper liners or lightly grease it.
2. **Mix Dry Ingredients:**
   - In a large bowl, whisk together the flour, granulated sugar, brown sugar, baking soda, baking powder, salt, cinnamon, and nutmeg.
3. **Mix Wet Ingredients:**
   - In another bowl, whisk together the melted butter, milk, eggs, and vanilla extract until well combined.
4. **Combine Ingredients:**
   - Pour the wet ingredients into the dry ingredients and gently fold together until just combined. Be careful not to overmix.
   - Gently fold in the diced apples.
5. **Fill Muffin Cups:**
   - Divide the batter evenly among the 12 muffin cups, filling each about 2/3 full.
6. **Prepare the Cinnamon Sugar Topping:**

- In a small bowl, mix together the granulated sugar and ground cinnamon.
- Brush the tops of the muffin batter with melted butter, then sprinkle generously with the cinnamon sugar mixture.

7. **Bake:**
    - Bake in the preheated oven for 18-22 minutes, or until a toothpick inserted into the center of a muffin comes out clean.
8. **Cool:**
    - Allow the muffins to cool in the pan for 5 minutes before transferring them to a wire rack to cool completely.

Tips:

- **Apple Selection:** Use firm apples that hold their shape well when baked, such as Granny Smith or Honeycrisp.
- **Dicing Apples:** Make sure to dice the apples into small, even pieces so they distribute well throughout the batter.
- **Mixing:** Avoid overmixing the batter to keep the muffins light and fluffy.

These Cinnamon Apple Muffins are a perfect way to enjoy the flavors of cinnamon and apples in a convenient, handheld treat. They're great fresh out of the oven or enjoyed later in the day!

Cinnamon Swirl Bread

Ingredients:

For the Dough:

- 1 cup warm milk (110°F or 45°C)
- 1/4 cup granulated sugar
- 2 1/4 tsp active dry yeast (1 packet)
- 1/4 cup unsalted butter, softened
- 1/2 tsp salt
- 2 large eggs
- 4 cups all-purpose flour (plus extra for dusting)

For the Cinnamon Swirl:

- 1/2 cup granulated sugar
- 1 tbsp ground cinnamon
- 2 tbsp unsalted butter, melted

For the Glaze (optional):

- 1/2 cup powdered sugar
- 1-2 tbsp milk
- 1/2 tsp vanilla extract

Instructions:

1. **Prepare the Yeast:**
   - In a small bowl, combine the warm milk and granulated sugar. Sprinkle the yeast over the top and let it sit for about 5-10 minutes until frothy.
2. **Mix the Dough:**
   - In a large mixing bowl, combine 3 1/2 cups of flour and salt.
   - Add the yeast mixture, softened butter, and eggs to the flour mixture.
   - Mix until the dough begins to come together. Gradually add the remaining 1/2 cup of flour as needed until the dough is soft but not sticky.
3. **Knead and Rise:**
   - Turn the dough out onto a floured surface and knead for about 5-7 minutes until smooth and elastic.
   - Place the dough in a greased bowl, cover with plastic wrap or a damp cloth, and let it rise in a warm place for about 1 hour, or until doubled in size.
4. **Prepare the Cinnamon Swirl:**
   - In a small bowl, mix together the granulated sugar and ground cinnamon. Set aside.
5. **Shape the Dough:**

- Punch down the risen dough and turn it out onto a floured surface. Roll it out into a rectangle about 12x18 inches.
- Brush the melted butter over the dough.
- Evenly sprinkle the cinnamon sugar mixture over the buttered dough.

6. **Roll and Shape:**
   - Starting from the long edge, carefully roll the dough into a tight log.
   - Pinch the seam to seal and place the rolled dough seam-side down in a greased 9x5-inch loaf pan.

7. **Second Rise:**
   - Cover the loaf pan with a damp cloth or plastic wrap and let it rise in a warm place for about 30-45 minutes, or until the dough has risen and is just above the rim of the pan.

8. **Bake:**
   - Preheat the oven to 350°F (175°C).
   - Bake the bread for 30-35 minutes, or until the loaf is golden brown and sounds hollow when tapped on the bottom.

9. **Cool and Glaze:**
   - Allow the bread to cool in the pan for 10 minutes before transferring it to a wire rack to cool completely.
   - If using the glaze, whisk together the powdered sugar, milk, and vanilla extract until smooth. Drizzle over the cooled bread.

Tips:

- **Flour:** Be careful not to add too much flour; the dough should be soft but manageable.
- **Rising:** Ensure the dough is in a warm, draft-free area to rise effectively.
- **Swirl Distribution:** For a more pronounced swirl, you can fold the dough over itself before placing it in the loaf pan.

This Cinnamon Swirl Bread is a comforting and delicious addition to any meal or a treat on its own. Enjoy the wonderful aroma and taste of homemade cinnamon bread!

Cinnamon Streusel Coffee Cake

Ingredients:

For the Cake:

- 2 1/2 cups all-purpose flour
- 1 1/2 tsp baking powder
- 1/2 tsp baking soda
- 1/2 tsp salt
- 1 cup unsalted butter, softened
- 1 cup granulated sugar
- 1/2 cup brown sugar, packed
- 2 large eggs
- 1 cup sour cream or plain Greek yogurt
- 1 tsp vanilla extract

For the Cinnamon Streusel Topping:

- 1/2 cup granulated sugar
- 1/2 cup packed brown sugar
- 1/2 cup all-purpose flour
- 1 tbsp ground cinnamon
- 1/4 cup unsalted butter, cold and cut into small pieces

For the Glaze (optional):

- 1/2 cup powdered sugar
- 1-2 tbsp milk
- 1/2 tsp vanilla extract

Instructions:

1. **Prepare the Oven and Pan:**
    - Preheat your oven to 350°F (175°C). Grease and flour a 9-inch round or square baking pan, or line it with parchment paper.
2. **Prepare the Streusel Topping:**
    - In a medium bowl, combine the granulated sugar, brown sugar, flour, and cinnamon.
    - Cut in the cold butter using a pastry cutter or your fingers until the mixture resembles coarse crumbs. Set aside.
3. **Mix the Cake Batter:**
    - In a large bowl, whisk together the flour, baking powder, baking soda, and salt.
    - In another bowl, beat the softened butter, granulated sugar, and brown sugar until light and fluffy.

- Add the eggs one at a time, beating well after each addition. Mix in the vanilla extract.
- Gradually add the dry ingredients to the butter mixture, alternating with the sour cream (or yogurt), beginning and ending with the dry ingredients. Mix until just combined.

4. **Assemble the Cake:**
    - Spread half of the cake batter evenly in the prepared pan.
    - Sprinkle about half of the streusel topping evenly over the batter.
    - Spread the remaining batter over the streusel layer, and then sprinkle the remaining streusel on top.
5. **Bake:**
    - Bake in the preheated oven for 40-45 minutes, or until a toothpick inserted into the center of the cake comes out clean and the top is golden brown.
6. **Cool and Glaze:**
    - Allow the cake to cool in the pan for about 10 minutes before transferring it to a wire rack to cool completely.
    - If using the glaze, whisk together the powdered sugar, milk, and vanilla extract until smooth. Drizzle over the cooled cake.

Tips:

- **Butter Temperature:** Ensure the butter is softened for the cake batter and cold for the streusel topping to get the right texture.
- **Mixing:** Be careful not to overmix the batter to keep the cake tender.
- **Storage:** Store the coffee cake in an airtight container at room temperature for up to 3 days or refrigerate for longer storage.

This Cinnamon Streusel Coffee Cake is a perfect blend of sweet, spiced flavors and a crumbly topping, making it a delicious choice for any occasion!

Cinnamon Oatmeal Cookies

Ingredients:

- 1 cup unsalted butter, softened
- 1 cup granulated sugar
- 1 cup packed brown sugar
- 2 large eggs
- 1 tsp vanilla extract
- 1 1/2 cups all-purpose flour
- 1 tsp baking soda
- 1/2 tsp baking powder
- 1/2 tsp salt
- 1 tbsp ground cinnamon
- 3 cups old-fashioned rolled oats
- 1 cup raisins or chocolate chips (optional)

Instructions:

1. **Prepare the Oven and Baking Sheets:**
   - Preheat your oven to 350°F (175°C). Line two baking sheets with parchment paper or silicone baking mats.
2. **Mix the Wet Ingredients:**
   - In a large bowl, beat the softened butter, granulated sugar, and brown sugar until light and fluffy.
   - Add the eggs one at a time, beating well after each addition. Mix in the vanilla extract.
3. **Combine Dry Ingredients:**
   - In another bowl, whisk together the flour, baking soda, baking powder, salt, and ground cinnamon.
4. **Mix Wet and Dry Ingredients:**
   - Gradually add the dry ingredients to the wet ingredients, mixing until combined.
   - Stir in the oats and, if using, the raisins or chocolate chips.
5. **Shape the Cookies:**
   - Drop rounded tablespoons of dough onto the prepared baking sheets, spacing them about 2 inches apart.
6. **Bake:**
   - Bake in the preheated oven for 10-12 minutes, or until the edges are golden brown but the centers are still soft.
7. **Cool:**
   - Allow the cookies to cool on the baking sheets for a few minutes before transferring them to a wire rack to cool completely.

Tips:

- **Butter:** Make sure the butter is softened to room temperature for easy mixing.
- **Oats:** Use old-fashioned rolled oats for the best texture. Quick oats can be used but may result in a slightly different texture.
- **Mix-ins:** Customize your cookies by adding nuts, dried fruit, or chocolate chips if desired.

These Cinnamon Oatmeal Cookies are a delightful treat with a perfect balance of chewy oats and spicy cinnamon. Enjoy them fresh from the oven or as a tasty snack anytime!

Cinnamon French Toast

Ingredients:

- 4 large eggs
- 1 cup milk
- 1/4 cup heavy cream
- 2 tbsp granulated sugar
- 1 tsp vanilla extract
- 1 tsp ground cinnamon
- 1/4 tsp ground nutmeg (optional)
- 8 slices of bread (preferably a day or two old; brioche, challah, or sourdough work well)
- 2 tbsp unsalted butter (for cooking)
- Maple syrup, powdered sugar, and fresh berries (for serving, optional)

Instructions:

1. **Prepare the Custard:**
    - In a large bowl, whisk together the eggs, milk, heavy cream, granulated sugar, vanilla extract, ground cinnamon, and ground nutmeg (if using) until well combined.
2. **Preheat the Pan:**
    - Heat a large skillet or griddle over medium heat. Add 1 tablespoon of butter and let it melt, swirling it around to coat the pan.
3. **Dip the Bread:**
    - Dip each slice of bread into the egg mixture, ensuring it is fully coated. Allow any excess custard to drip off.
4. **Cook the French Toast:**
    - Place the dipped bread slices in the skillet or on the griddle. Cook for about 2-3 minutes per side, or until golden brown and cooked through.
5. **Keep Warm (Optional):**
    - If cooking in batches, keep the cooked French toast warm by placing it on a baking sheet in a preheated oven at 200°F (95°C) while you finish cooking the remaining slices.
6. **Serve:**
    - Serve the French toast warm with your favorite toppings, such as maple syrup, a dusting of powdered sugar, and fresh berries.

Tips:

- **Bread:** Stale or slightly dry bread works best as it soaks up the custard without becoming too soggy. If your bread is fresh, you can lightly toast it before dipping.
- **Butter:** Use enough butter to coat the pan between batches to prevent sticking and to give the French toast a nice golden color.

- **Customizing:** Add a pinch of salt to the custard mixture for enhanced flavor, or try adding a splash of orange zest for a different twist.

Enjoy your Cinnamon French Toast with a variety of toppings for a delicious and satisfying breakfast!

Cinnamon Pear Compote

Ingredients:

- 4 ripe pears (such as Bartlett or Anjou), peeled, cored, and diced
- 1/4 cup granulated sugar (adjust to taste depending on the sweetness of the pears)
- 1/4 cup water or apple juice
- 1 tsp ground cinnamon
- 1/4 tsp ground nutmeg (optional)
- 1 tbsp lemon juice (optional, for a touch of brightness)
- 1/2 tsp vanilla extract (optional)

Instructions:

1. **Prepare the Pears:**
   - Peel, core, and dice the pears into small chunks.
2. **Cook the Compote:**
   - In a medium saucepan, combine the diced pears, granulated sugar, and water (or apple juice).
   - Stir in the ground cinnamon and nutmeg (if using).
3. **Simmer:**
   - Bring the mixture to a simmer over medium heat.
   - Reduce the heat to low and cook for about 10-15 minutes, or until the pears are tender and the liquid has thickened slightly. Stir occasionally.
4. **Add Finishing Touches:**
   - If using, stir in the lemon juice and vanilla extract.
   - Adjust the sweetness or spice level to taste, adding more sugar or cinnamon if desired.
5. **Cool and Serve:**
   - Allow the compote to cool slightly before serving. It can be served warm or at room temperature.

Tips:

- **Pears:** Use ripe but firm pears to ensure they hold their shape while cooking. Overripe pears may become too mushy.
- **Texture:** For a smoother texture, you can mash the pears with a fork or potato masher after cooking.
- **Storage:** Store any leftover compote in an airtight container in the refrigerator for up to a week. It can also be frozen for longer storage.

This Cinnamon Pear Compote is versatile and can be used to add a touch of warmth and spice to many dishes. Enjoy it on breakfast favorites, as a topping for desserts, or even stirred into oatmeal for added flavor!

Cinnamon Raisin Bagels

Ingredients:

For the Bagels:

- 4 cups all-purpose flour
- 1 tbsp granulated sugar
- 2 tsp ground cinnamon
- 1 tsp salt
- 2 1/4 tsp active dry yeast (1 packet)
- 1 1/4 cups warm water (110°F or 45°C)
- 1/2 cup raisins
- 1 tbsp honey (for boiling)

For the Topping:

- 1 tbsp granulated sugar
- 1 tsp ground cinnamon

Instructions:

1. **Prepare the Dough:**
    - In a small bowl, dissolve the yeast in the warm water and let it sit for about 5-10 minutes until frothy.
    - In a large mixing bowl, combine the flour, granulated sugar, ground cinnamon, and salt.
    - Add the yeast mixture to the dry ingredients and mix until a dough forms. Knead the dough on a floured surface for about 8-10 minutes until smooth and elastic.
2. **Add the Raisins:**
    - Gently fold the raisins into the dough until evenly distributed.
3. **First Rise:**
    - Place the dough in a greased bowl, cover with plastic wrap or a damp cloth, and let it rise in a warm place for about 1 hour, or until doubled in size.
4. **Shape the Bagels:**
    - Punch down the dough and turn it out onto a floured surface. Divide the dough into 8 equal pieces.
    - Roll each piece into a ball, then use your thumb to make a hole in the center and stretch it to form a bagel shape. Alternatively, you can roll the dough into a rope and shape it into a ring, pinching the ends together.
5. **Prepare for Boiling:**
    - Preheat your oven to 425°F (220°C).
    - Bring a large pot of water to a boil and stir in the honey.

- Carefully drop the bagels into the boiling water, cooking for about 1-2 minutes on each side. Use a slotted spoon to remove the bagels and place them on a parchment-lined baking sheet.
6. **Add the Topping:**
    - In a small bowl, mix the granulated sugar and ground cinnamon. Sprinkle this mixture over the top of each bagel.
7. **Bake:**
    - Bake the bagels in the preheated oven for 20-25 minutes, or until golden brown and cooked through.
8. **Cool:**
    - Allow the bagels to cool on a wire rack before slicing.

Tips:

- **Yeast:** Ensure the water is warm but not hot to avoid killing the yeast.
- **Shaping:** When shaping the bagels, make sure the hole in the center is large enough, as it can shrink during boiling and baking.
- **Boiling:** Boiling the bagels gives them their distinctive texture and helps them rise properly in the oven.

Enjoy these Cinnamon Raisin Bagels fresh out of the oven with a spread of cream cheese, or toasted with a bit of butter. They're a tasty and satisfying addition to any meal!

Cinnamon Spiced Nuts

Ingredients:

- 2 cups mixed nuts (such as almonds, pecans, walnuts, and cashews)
- 2 tbsp unsalted butter, melted
- 1/4 cup granulated sugar
- 1 tbsp ground cinnamon
- 1/4 tsp ground nutmeg (optional)
- 1/4 tsp salt
- 1 tbsp honey or maple syrup (optional, for extra sweetness)

Instructions:

1. **Preheat the Oven:**
   - Preheat your oven to 350°F (175°C). Line a baking sheet with parchment paper or a silicone baking mat.
2. **Prepare the Nuts:**
   - In a large bowl, combine the nuts and melted butter. Toss to coat the nuts evenly.
3. **Mix the Spices:**
   - In a small bowl, mix together the granulated sugar, ground cinnamon, ground nutmeg (if using), and salt.
4. **Coat the Nuts:**
   - Sprinkle the spice mixture over the nuts and toss until they are evenly coated. If using honey or maple syrup, drizzle it over the nuts and toss again to coat.
5. **Bake:**
   - Spread the coated nuts in an even layer on the prepared baking sheet.
   - Bake in the preheated oven for 10-15 minutes, stirring once or twice, until the nuts are golden brown and fragrant. Be careful not to overbake, as the nuts can quickly become burnt.
6. **Cool:**
   - Remove the nuts from the oven and let them cool completely on the baking sheet. They will become crisp as they cool.
7. **Store:**
   - Once cooled, store the nuts in an airtight container at room temperature for up to 2 weeks.

Tips:

- **Nuts:** Feel free to use any variety of nuts you prefer or have on hand.
- **Stirring:** Stirring the nuts during baking ensures they cook evenly and don't burn.
- **Sweetness:** Adjust the amount of sugar or honey/maple syrup based on your preference for sweetness.

These Cinnamon Spiced Nuts make for a great snack and are also perfect for gifting during the holidays. Enjoy their crunchy texture and warm, spiced flavor!

Cinnamon Maple Granola

Ingredients:

- 3 cups old-fashioned rolled oats
- 1 cup nuts and seeds (such as almonds, walnuts, pecans, sunflower seeds, or pumpkin seeds), chopped if large
- 1/2 cup unsweetened shredded coconut (optional)
- 1/2 cup pure maple syrup
- 1/4 cup coconut oil or olive oil
- 1/4 cup brown sugar or coconut sugar
- 1 tsp ground cinnamon
- 1/4 tsp salt
- 1/2 cup dried fruit (such as raisins, cranberries, or chopped dried apricots), optional

Instructions:

1. **Preheat the Oven:**
   - Preheat your oven to 350°F (175°C). Line a large baking sheet with parchment paper or a silicone baking mat.
2. **Mix Dry Ingredients:**
   - In a large bowl, combine the rolled oats, chopped nuts and seeds, and shredded coconut (if using).
3. **Prepare the Wet Mixture:**
   - In a small saucepan, combine the maple syrup, coconut oil, brown sugar, ground cinnamon, and salt.
   - Heat over medium heat, stirring occasionally, until the mixture is well combined and the sugar is dissolved. Remove from heat.
4. **Combine Ingredients:**
   - Pour the wet mixture over the dry ingredients and stir until everything is evenly coated.
5. **Bake:**
   - Spread the granola mixture in an even layer on the prepared baking sheet.
   - Bake in the preheated oven for 20-25 minutes, stirring halfway through, until the granola is golden brown and fragrant. Be careful not to overbake, as granola can burn quickly.
6. **Add Dried Fruit:**
   - If using dried fruit, stir it into the granola immediately after removing it from the oven while it's still warm.
7. **Cool:**
   - Allow the granola to cool completely on the baking sheet. It will become crisp as it cools.
8. **Store:**
   - Store the cooled granola in an airtight container at room temperature for up to 2 weeks.

Tips:

- **Nuts and Seeds:** Customize the granola with your favorite nuts and seeds. Just be sure to chop larger pieces for even cooking.
- **Coconut:** If you don't like shredded coconut, you can leave it out or substitute with additional nuts and seeds.
- **Sweetness:** Adjust the amount of maple syrup and brown sugar to your taste. For a less sweet version, reduce the sugar.

This Cinnamon Maple Granola is a versatile and flavorful addition to your breakfast routine or a tasty snack option. Enjoy it with yogurt, milk, or just by the handful!

Cinnamon Chocolate Chip Scones

Ingredients:

For the Scones:

- 2 1/2 cups all-purpose flour
- 1/4 cup granulated sugar
- 1 tbsp baking powder
- 1/2 tsp salt
- 1 tsp ground cinnamon
- 1/2 cup cold unsalted butter, cut into small cubes
- 3/4 cup semi-sweet chocolate chips
- 1 cup whole milk or heavy cream
- 1 large egg

For the Glaze (optional):

- 1/2 cup powdered sugar
- 1-2 tbsp milk
- 1/4 tsp vanilla extract

Instructions:

1. **Preheat the Oven:**
    - Preheat your oven to 400°F (200°C). Line a baking sheet with parchment paper or a silicone baking mat.
2. **Prepare the Dry Ingredients:**
    - In a large bowl, whisk together the flour, granulated sugar, baking powder, salt, and ground cinnamon.
3. **Cut in the Butter:**
    - Add the cold butter cubes to the flour mixture. Use a pastry cutter or your fingers to cut the butter into the flour until the mixture resembles coarse crumbs with small pea-sized pieces of butter.
4. **Add Chocolate Chips:**
    - Stir in the chocolate chips.
5. **Combine Wet Ingredients:**
    - In a separate bowl, whisk together the milk (or heavy cream) and egg until well combined.
6. **Mix the Dough:**
    - Pour the wet ingredients into the dry ingredients and gently mix until just combined. The dough will be somewhat sticky.
7. **Shape the Scones:**

- Turn the dough out onto a floured surface and gently knead it a few times until it comes together. Pat the dough into a 1-inch thick circle or rectangle. Cut into 8-10 wedges or squares.
8. **Bake:**
    - Transfer the scones to the prepared baking sheet, spacing them a bit apart. Bake for 15-18 minutes, or until the scones are golden brown and a toothpick inserted into the center comes out clean.
9. **Cool and Glaze:**
    - Allow the scones to cool on the baking sheet for a few minutes before transferring them to a wire rack to cool completely.
    - If using the glaze, whisk together the powdered sugar, milk, and vanilla extract until smooth. Drizzle over the cooled scones.

Tips:

- **Butter:** Ensure the butter is cold to achieve a light, flaky texture.
- **Cutting the Dough:** For best results, avoid overworking the dough. The scones should be handled as little as possible.
- **Customizing:** You can substitute the chocolate chips with other mix-ins like dried fruit or nuts if desired.

Enjoy these Cinnamon Chocolate Chip Scones fresh out of the oven or toasted with a pat of butter. They're sure to be a hit with anyone who loves a sweet and spicy treat!

Cinnamon Apple Crumble

Ingredients:

For the Apple Filling:

- 6-7 medium apples (such as Granny Smith, Honeycrisp, or Braeburn), peeled, cored, and sliced
- 1/2 cup granulated sugar
- 1/4 cup packed brown sugar
- 1 tbsp lemon juice
- 1 tsp ground cinnamon
- 1/4 tsp ground nutmeg (optional)
- 1/4 cup all-purpose flour

For the Crumble Topping:

- 1 cup all-purpose flour
- 1/2 cup granulated sugar
- 1/2 cup packed brown sugar
- 1 tsp ground cinnamon
- 1/4 tsp salt
- 1/2 cup unsalted butter, cold and cut into small cubes
- 1/2 cup old-fashioned rolled oats

Instructions:

1. **Preheat the Oven:**
    - Preheat your oven to 350°F (175°C). Grease a 9x13-inch baking dish or a similar-sized ovenproof dish.
2. **Prepare the Apple Filling:**
    - In a large bowl, combine the sliced apples, granulated sugar, brown sugar, lemon juice, ground cinnamon, ground nutmeg (if using), and flour. Toss until the apples are evenly coated.
3. **Prepare the Crumble Topping:**
    - In a separate bowl, combine the flour, granulated sugar, brown sugar, ground cinnamon, and salt.
    - Add the cold butter cubes to the dry ingredients. Use a pastry cutter or your fingers to cut the butter into the mixture until it resembles coarse crumbs.
    - Stir in the rolled oats.
4. **Assemble the Crumble:**
    - Spread the apple mixture evenly in the prepared baking dish.
    - Sprinkle the crumble topping evenly over the apples.
5. **Bake:**

- Bake in the preheated oven for 45-55 minutes, or until the topping is golden brown and the apples are tender and bubbling.
6. **Cool and Serve:**
    - Allow the crumble to cool slightly before serving. It's delicious served warm, with a scoop of vanilla ice cream or a dollop of whipped cream if desired.

Tips:

- **Apple Variety:** Use a mix of tart and sweet apples for a balanced flavor. Granny Smith apples are particularly good for baking due to their tartness and firmness.
- **Butter:** Ensure the butter is cold for a crumbly topping.
- **Serving:** For a special treat, serve the crumble with a scoop of vanilla ice cream or a drizzle of caramel sauce.

Enjoy this Cinnamon Apple Crumble as a comforting dessert that's sure to please your family and friends!

Cinnamon Pumpkin Bread

Ingredients:

For the Bread:

- 1 1/2 cups all-purpose flour
- 1 cup granulated sugar
- 1/2 cup packed brown sugar
- 1/2 cup vegetable oil or melted butter
- 1 cup canned pumpkin puree (not pumpkin pie filling)
- 2 large eggs
- 1/4 cup water or milk
- 1 tsp vanilla extract
- 1 tsp ground cinnamon
- 1/2 tsp ground nutmeg
- 1/2 tsp ground ginger
- 1/2 tsp salt
- 1 1/2 tsp baking powder
- 1/2 tsp baking soda

For the Cinnamon Sugar Topping (optional):

- 2 tbsp granulated sugar
- 1 tsp ground cinnamon

Instructions:

1. **Preheat the Oven:**
   - Preheat your oven to 350°F (175°C). Grease and flour a 9x5-inch loaf pan or line it with parchment paper.
2. **Mix Dry Ingredients:**
   - In a medium bowl, whisk together the flour, granulated sugar, brown sugar, ground cinnamon, ground nutmeg, ground ginger, salt, baking powder, and baking soda.
3. **Mix Wet Ingredients:**
   - In a large bowl, combine the oil (or melted butter), pumpkin puree, eggs, water (or milk), and vanilla extract. Whisk until well combined.
4. **Combine Ingredients:**
   - Gradually add the dry ingredients to the wet ingredients, stirring until just combined. Do not overmix; the batter should be thick and a bit lumpy.
5. **Pour into Pan:**
   - Pour the batter into the prepared loaf pan and spread it evenly.
6. **Prepare the Topping (if using):**

- In a small bowl, mix the granulated sugar and ground cinnamon. Sprinkle this mixture evenly over the top of the batter.
7. **Bake:**
    - Bake in the preheated oven for 60-70 minutes, or until a toothpick inserted into the center of the loaf comes out clean.
8. **Cool:**
    - Allow the bread to cool in the pan for 10 minutes, then transfer it to a wire rack to cool completely before slicing.

Tips:

- **Pumpkin:** Use pure pumpkin puree rather than pumpkin pie filling, which contains added spices and sugar.
- **Oil vs. Butter:** Both oil and melted butter work well, but oil will result in a slightly moister bread.
- **Spices:** Adjust the spices to your taste. You can add more cinnamon, nutmeg, or ginger if you like a stronger spice flavor.
- **Storage:** Store the cooled bread in an airtight container at room temperature for up to a week, or freeze for up to 3 months.

This Cinnamon Pumpkin Bread is a delightful and cozy treat that brings the flavors of fall to your kitchen year-round. Enjoy it fresh or toasted with a bit of butter!

Cinnamon Sugar Pretzels

Ingredients:

For the Pretzels:

- 1 1/2 cups warm water (110°F or 45°C)
- 2 tbsp granulated sugar
- 2 1/4 tsp active dry yeast (1 packet)
- 4 cups all-purpose flour
- 1 tsp salt
- 1/4 cup baking soda
- 1 large egg, beaten (for egg wash)

For the Cinnamon Sugar Coating:

- 1/2 cup granulated sugar
- 1 tbsp ground cinnamon
- 2 tbsp unsalted butter, melted

Instructions:

1. **Prepare the Dough:**
   - In a large bowl, dissolve the sugar in the warm water. Sprinkle the yeast over the water and let it sit for about 5-10 minutes, until it becomes frothy.
   - In a separate large bowl, combine the flour and salt.
   - Add the yeast mixture to the flour mixture and stir until a dough forms. Knead the dough on a floured surface for about 5-7 minutes, until it's smooth and elastic.
2. **Let the Dough Rise:**
   - Place the dough in a greased bowl, cover with plastic wrap or a damp cloth, and let it rise in a warm place for about 1 hour, or until doubled in size.
3. **Preheat the Oven:**
   - Preheat your oven to 425°F (220°C). Line a baking sheet with parchment paper or a silicone baking mat.
4. **Shape the Pretzels:**
   - Punch down the dough and turn it out onto a floured surface. Divide the dough into 12 equal pieces.
   - Roll each piece into a long rope (about 18 inches in length). Shape each rope into a pretzel shape by forming a U, then crossing the ends over each other and pressing them down to form the pretzel shape.
5. **Prepare the Baking Soda Bath:**
   - In a large pot, bring 4 cups of water to a boil and stir in the baking soda.
   - Carefully dip each pretzel into the boiling water for about 30 seconds, then remove with a slotted spoon and place on the prepared baking sheet. Brush each pretzel with the beaten egg.

6. **Bake:**
    - Bake the pretzels in the preheated oven for 12-15 minutes, or until golden brown.
7. **Coat with Cinnamon Sugar:**
    - While the pretzels are baking, mix the granulated sugar and ground cinnamon in a small bowl.
    - Once the pretzels are out of the oven, immediately brush them with the melted butter and sprinkle generously with the cinnamon sugar mixture.
8. **Cool:**
    - Allow the pretzels to cool slightly on a wire rack before serving.

Tips:

- **Boiling Soda Bath:** The baking soda bath gives the pretzels their distinctive chewy texture and deep brown color. Don't skip this step.
- **Shaping:** Make sure to shape the pretzels evenly so they cook uniformly.
- **Topping:** For extra cinnamon sugar coating, you can roll the warm pretzels in the cinnamon sugar mixture if desired.

These Cinnamon Sugar Pretzels are a sweet and satisfying treat, perfect for enjoying with a cup of coffee or hot chocolate. They're best served fresh but can be reheated in the oven to restore their crispiness.

Cinnamon Cream Cheese Frosting

Ingredients:

- 8 oz (225 g) cream cheese, softened
- 1/2 cup (1 stick) unsalted butter, softened
- 3-4 cups powdered sugar, sifted (adjust to desired sweetness and consistency)
- 1 tsp ground cinnamon
- 1 tsp vanilla extract
- Pinch of salt (optional, to taste)

Instructions:

1. **Beat the Cream Cheese and Butter:**
   - In a large bowl, use an electric mixer to beat the softened cream cheese and butter together on medium speed until smooth and creamy.
2. **Add the Sugar and Spices:**
   - Gradually add the sifted powdered sugar, about 1 cup at a time, beating on low speed to incorporate the sugar into the cream cheese mixture. Increase to medium speed once the sugar is added.
   - Add the ground cinnamon and vanilla extract. Beat until the frosting is smooth and fluffy. If the frosting is too thick, you can add a little milk or cream, 1 teaspoon at a time, until you reach your desired consistency.
3. **Adjust the Sweetness:**
   - Taste the frosting and adjust the sweetness or cinnamon if needed. If you like a stronger cinnamon flavor, you can add a bit more ground cinnamon. If it's too sweet, a small pinch of salt can help balance the flavor.
4. **Frost Your Baked Goods:**
   - Once the frosting is ready, use it immediately to frost your cooled cakes, cupcakes, or other baked goods.
5. **Store:**
   - If you have leftover frosting, store it in an airtight container in the refrigerator for up to a week. Let it come to room temperature and re-whip briefly before using.

Tips:

- **Softening:** Ensure that both the cream cheese and butter are softened to room temperature for the smoothest frosting.
- **Consistency:** Adjust the consistency by adding more powdered sugar to thicken or a little milk/cream to thin it out.
- **Flavor Variations:** For a different twist, you can experiment with adding a small amount of maple syrup or other spices, like nutmeg, if you like.

This Cinnamon Cream Cheese Frosting is perfect for adding a delightful touch of sweetness and spice to your baked treats. Enjoy its creamy texture and warm cinnamon flavor!

Cinnamon Baked Apples

Ingredients:

- 4 medium apples (such as Granny Smith, Honeycrisp, or Fuji)
- 1/4 cup granulated sugar
- 1/4 cup packed brown sugar
- 1 tsp ground cinnamon
- 1/4 tsp ground nutmeg (optional)
- 1/4 cup unsalted butter, cut into small pieces
- 1/4 cup chopped nuts (such as walnuts or pecans) (optional)
- 1/4 cup raisins or dried cranberries (optional)
- 1/4 cup water or apple juice

Instructions:

1. **Preheat the Oven:**
   - Preheat your oven to 350°F (175°C).
2. **Prepare the Apples:**
   - Wash and core the apples, creating a hollow space in the center. You can use an apple corer or a knife to carefully remove the core, leaving the base intact to hold the filling.
3. **Make the Filling:**
   - In a small bowl, mix together the granulated sugar, brown sugar, ground cinnamon, and ground nutmeg (if using). If you're adding nuts and/or raisins, mix them into the sugar mixture.
4. **Stuff the Apples:**
   - Spoon the sugar mixture into the hollowed centers of the apples, packing it in lightly. Place a small piece of butter on top of each filled apple.
5. **Prepare for Baking:**
   - Place the stuffed apples in a baking dish. Pour the water or apple juice into the bottom of the dish to help create steam and keep the apples moist during baking.
6. **Bake:**
   - Bake in the preheated oven for 30-40 minutes, or until the apples are tender and the filling is bubbly. The baking time will depend on the size and type of apples used.
7. **Serve:**
   - Let the baked apples cool slightly before serving. They can be enjoyed warm on their own or with a scoop of vanilla ice cream or a dollop of whipped cream.

Tips:

- **Apple Variety:** Choose apples that are firm and hold their shape well during baking.
- **Texture:** For a more tender texture, bake the apples longer. If you prefer them slightly firmer, reduce the baking time.

- **Variation:** Experiment with different spices or add a touch of vanilla extract to the filling for added flavor.

Cinnamon Baked Apples make a warm, comforting dessert that highlights the natural sweetness of apples with a hint of spice. Enjoy this easy and delicious treat with your favorite toppings!

Cinnamon Sticky Buns

Ingredients:

For the Dough:

- 1 cup whole milk
- 1/2 cup granulated sugar
- 1/2 cup unsalted butter, plus extra for greasing
- 1 packet (2 1/4 tsp) active dry yeast
- 2 large eggs
- 4 cups all-purpose flour
- 1/2 tsp salt

For the Cinnamon Filling:

- 1/2 cup unsalted butter, softened
- 1 cup packed brown sugar
- 2 tbsp ground cinnamon
- 1/2 cup finely chopped nuts (such as pecans or walnuts) (optional)

For the Sticky Topping:

- 1/2 cup unsalted butter
- 1/2 cup packed brown sugar
- 1/4 cup honey or light corn syrup
- 1/2 cup chopped nuts (optional)

Instructions:

1. **Prepare the Dough:**
   - Warm the milk in a small saucepan until it's about 110°F (45°C). Remove from heat and stir in the granulated sugar until dissolved. Sprinkle the yeast over the milk and let it sit for about 5-10 minutes, or until frothy.
   - In a large bowl, whisk together the eggs and melted butter. Add the yeast mixture and mix well.
   - Gradually add the flour and salt, stirring until a soft dough forms. Turn the dough out onto a floured surface and knead for about 5-7 minutes, until smooth and elastic.
2. **Let the Dough Rise:**
   - Place the dough in a greased bowl, cover with plastic wrap or a damp cloth, and let it rise in a warm place for about 1 hour, or until doubled in size.
3. **Prepare the Filling:**
   - In a small bowl, mix the softened butter, brown sugar, and ground cinnamon until well combined.
4. **Assemble the Buns:**

- Punch down the risen dough and turn it out onto a floured surface. Roll the dough into a 16x12-inch rectangle.
- Spread the cinnamon filling evenly over the dough. Sprinkle with chopped nuts if using.
- Roll the dough tightly from the long side into a log. Slice the log into 12 equal pieces.

5. **Prepare the Sticky Topping:**
   - In a small saucepan, melt the butter over medium heat. Stir in the brown sugar and honey (or corn syrup) until smooth. Pour this mixture into the bottom of a greased 9x13-inch baking dish. Sprinkle with additional chopped nuts if desired.

6. **Arrange and Bake:**
   - Place the sliced buns cut side up in the prepared baking dish over the sticky topping. Cover and let rise in a warm place for about 30 minutes.
   - Preheat your oven to 350°F (175°C).
   - Bake the buns for 25-30 minutes, or until golden brown and cooked through.

7. **Cool and Serve:**
   - Let the sticky buns cool in the pan for about 10 minutes, then invert the pan onto a serving platter so the sticky topping is on top. Serve warm.

Tips:

- **Dough Consistency:** If the dough is too sticky, add a little more flour. If too dry, add a splash of milk.
- **Rising Time:** Ensure the dough is placed in a warm, draft-free area to rise properly.
- **Topping:** Be sure to pour the sticky topping into the pan before placing the buns in so it can coat them as they bake.

These Cinnamon Sticky Buns are wonderfully gooey and sweet, making them a fantastic treat to enjoy with family and friends.

Cinnamon Roll Waffles

Ingredients:

For the Waffles:

- 1 can (12.4 oz) refrigerated cinnamon rolls with icing (like Pillsbury)
- 1/4 cup milk (or as needed for consistency)
- 1 tsp ground cinnamon (optional, for extra flavor)
- 1/2 tsp vanilla extract (optional)

For the Icing:

- Reserved icing from the cinnamon roll can
- 1/4 cup powdered sugar (optional, if extra icing is needed)
- 1-2 tbsp milk (for thinning the icing, if needed)

Instructions:

1. **Preheat the Waffle Iron:**
   - Preheat your waffle iron according to the manufacturer's instructions.
2. **Prepare the Cinnamon Roll Batter:**
   - Open the can of refrigerated cinnamon rolls. Separate the rolls and cut them into smaller pieces (about 4-6 pieces per roll).
   - In a bowl, mix the cinnamon roll pieces with a splash of milk to make them more spreadable. You may also add ground cinnamon and vanilla extract to enhance the flavor if desired.
3. **Cook the Waffles:**
   - Lightly grease the waffle iron with non-stick spray or a small amount of oil.
   - Place the cinnamon roll pieces in the preheated waffle iron, spreading them out evenly. Close the waffle iron and cook for about 4-5 minutes, or until the waffles are golden brown and cooked through. The cooking time may vary depending on your waffle iron.
4. **Prepare the Icing:**
   - While the waffles are cooking, heat the reserved icing from the cinnamon roll can in the microwave for about 10-15 seconds to make it easier to drizzle. If you need additional icing, mix the powdered sugar with milk until smooth and desired consistency is achieved.
5. **Serve:**
   - Once the cinnamon roll waffles are cooked, remove them from the waffle iron and place them on a serving plate.
   - Drizzle with the warmed icing. You can also add any additional toppings you like, such as fresh fruit, nuts, or a sprinkle of powdered sugar.

Tips:

- **Consistency:** If the cinnamon roll batter is too thick, add a little more milk to thin it out. It should spread evenly but not be too runny.
- **Waffle Iron:** Make sure not to overcrowd the waffle iron. If you have a large batch, cook the waffles in batches.
- **Serving:** These waffles are best served warm. If you have leftovers, reheat them in a toaster or oven to restore their crispy texture.

Cinnamon Roll Waffles are a delightful and creative breakfast treat that combines the best aspects of cinnamon rolls and waffles. Enjoy them fresh with your favorite toppings for a delicious start to your day!

Cinnamon Coffee Cake Muffins

Ingredients:

For the Muffins:

- 2 1/2 cups all-purpose flour
- 1 cup granulated sugar
- 1/2 cup packed brown sugar
- 1/2 cup unsalted butter, melted
- 1 cup milk (whole milk or 2% is best)
- 2 large eggs
- 1 tbsp baking powder
- 1/2 tsp salt
- 1 tsp ground cinnamon
- 1 tsp vanilla extract

For the Cinnamon Swirl:

- 1/2 cup granulated sugar
- 1 tbsp ground cinnamon

For the Streusel Topping:

- 1/2 cup all-purpose flour
- 1/4 cup granulated sugar
- 1/4 cup packed brown sugar
- 1/4 cup unsalted butter, cold and cut into small pieces
- 1/2 tsp ground cinnamon

Instructions:

1. **Preheat the Oven:**
   - Preheat your oven to 375°F (190°C). Line a muffin tin with paper liners or grease the muffin cups.
2. **Prepare the Cinnamon Swirl:**
   - In a small bowl, mix together the granulated sugar and ground cinnamon. Set aside.
3. **Prepare the Streusel Topping:**
   - In another bowl, combine the flour, granulated sugar, brown sugar, and ground cinnamon. Add the cold butter pieces and use a pastry cutter or your fingers to work the butter into the mixture until it resembles coarse crumbs. Set aside.
4. **Mix the Muffin Batter:**
   - In a large bowl, whisk together the flour, granulated sugar, baking powder, and salt.
   - In a separate bowl, mix the melted butter, milk, eggs, and vanilla extract.

- Gradually add the wet ingredients to the dry ingredients, stirring until just combined. Do not overmix; the batter should be a bit lumpy.
5. **Assemble the Muffins:**
    - Spoon a small amount of batter into each muffin cup (about 1/3 full).
    - Sprinkle a teaspoon of the cinnamon sugar mixture over the batter.
    - Top with more batter, filling the cups about 2/3 full.
    - Sprinkle the remaining cinnamon sugar mixture on top of the batter.
6. **Add the Streusel Topping:**
    - Sprinkle the streusel topping evenly over each muffin.
7. **Bake:**
    - Bake in the preheated oven for 18-22 minutes, or until a toothpick inserted into the center comes out clean and the tops are golden brown.
8. **Cool and Serve:**
    - Allow the muffins to cool in the pan for 5 minutes before transferring them to a wire rack to cool completely.

Tips:

- **Consistency:** Be careful not to overmix the muffin batter; this can make the muffins dense.
- **Butter:** For a better texture, make sure the butter is melted but not too hot when adding to the batter.
- **Storage:** Store cooled muffins in an airtight container at room temperature for up to 3 days or freeze for longer storage.

Cinnamon Coffee Cake Muffins are a delightful treat with a rich, buttery flavor and a sweet cinnamon swirl. They're perfect for a breakfast on the go or a special weekend brunch. Enjoy!

Cinnamon Sugar Popcorn

Ingredients:

- 1/2 cup popcorn kernels (or about 12 cups popped popcorn)
- 1/4 cup unsalted butter (1/2 stick)
- 1/2 cup granulated sugar
- 1 tsp ground cinnamon
- 1/4 tsp salt (optional, to enhance flavor)
- 1/4 cup powdered sugar (optional, for extra sweetness and to help the cinnamon sugar stick)

Instructions:

1. **Pop the Popcorn:**
   - Pop the popcorn kernels using an air popper, stovetop, or microwave according to the manufacturer's instructions. Place the popped popcorn in a large bowl, making sure to remove any unpopped kernels.
2. **Prepare the Cinnamon Sugar Coating:**
   - In a small bowl, mix together the granulated sugar, ground cinnamon, and salt (if using). Set aside.
3. **Melt the Butter:**
   - In a small saucepan, melt the butter over medium heat. Once melted, remove from heat.
4. **Coat the Popcorn:**
   - Pour the melted butter over the popped popcorn, tossing gently to coat evenly.
   - Sprinkle the cinnamon sugar mixture over the buttered popcorn, tossing again to ensure the popcorn is evenly coated.
5. **Optional: Add Powdered Sugar:**
   - For extra sweetness and to help the coating stick better, sift the powdered sugar over the coated popcorn and toss gently.
6. **Cool and Serve:**
   - Allow the cinnamon sugar popcorn to cool slightly before serving. The coating will become crisp as it cools.

Tips:

- **Even Coating:** For the best results, ensure that the popcorn is still warm when adding the butter and cinnamon sugar. This helps the coating adhere better.
- **Storage:** Store any leftover popcorn in an airtight container at room temperature for up to a week. It may lose some crispness over time but will still be delicious.

This Cinnamon Sugar Popcorn is a delightful treat that's easy to make and perfect for satisfying your sweet tooth with a crunchy twist. Enjoy it as a fun snack or a special treat!

Cinnamon Swirl Pancakes

Ingredients:

For the Pancakes:

- 1 1/2 cups all-purpose flour
- 2 tbsp granulated sugar
- 1 tbsp baking powder
- 1/2 tsp salt
- 1 1/4 cups milk (whole milk or 2% is best)
- 1 large egg
- 3 tbsp unsalted butter, melted
- 1 tsp vanilla extract

For the Cinnamon Swirl:

- 1/4 cup unsalted butter, melted
- 1/2 cup brown sugar, packed
- 1 tbsp ground cinnamon

Optional: For Serving

- Maple syrup
- Powdered sugar
- Whipped cream

Instructions:

1. **Prepare the Cinnamon Swirl:**
    - In a small bowl, mix together the melted butter, brown sugar, and ground cinnamon until well combined. Set aside.
2. **Make the Pancake Batter:**
    - In a large bowl, whisk together the flour, granulated sugar, baking powder, and salt.
    - In a separate bowl, whisk the milk, egg, melted butter, and vanilla extract until combined.
    - Pour the wet ingredients into the dry ingredients and stir until just combined. The batter will be lumpy, and that's okay. Do not overmix.
3. **Cook the Pancakes:**
    - Preheat a griddle or non-stick skillet over medium heat. Lightly grease with butter or cooking spray.
    - For each pancake, pour about 1/4 cup of batter onto the griddle. Using a spoon or knife, drizzle a swirl of the cinnamon mixture over the top of the batter. Use a toothpick or skewer to gently swirl the cinnamon mixture into the pancake batter, creating a marbled effect.

- Cook until bubbles form on the surface of the pancake and the edges look set, about 2-3 minutes. Flip and cook for another 1-2 minutes, or until golden brown and cooked through.
4. **Serve:**
    - Serve the cinnamon swirl pancakes warm, topped with maple syrup, a dusting of powdered sugar, and whipped cream if desired.

Tips:

- **Heat:** Make sure your griddle or skillet is well-heated before cooking the pancakes to ensure they cook evenly.
- **Swirling:** Don't overmix the cinnamon swirl into the batter; you want to keep the marbled effect.
- **Consistency:** If the cinnamon swirl mixture is too thick, you can add a little more melted butter to thin it out.

Cinnamon Swirl Pancakes are a delicious and visually appealing breakfast option that combines the comforting flavors of cinnamon rolls with the classic pancake. Enjoy them with your favorite toppings for a delightful treat!

Cinnamon Pecan Sticky Buns

Ingredients:

For the Dough:

- 1 cup whole milk
- 1/4 cup granulated sugar
- 1/4 cup unsalted butter
- 1 packet (2 1/4 tsp) active dry yeast
- 2 large eggs
- 4 cups all-purpose flour
- 1/2 tsp salt

For the Cinnamon Filling:

- 1/2 cup unsalted butter, softened
- 1 cup packed brown sugar
- 2 tbsp ground cinnamon
- 1/2 cup chopped pecans

For the Sticky Topping:

- 1/2 cup unsalted butter
- 1/2 cup packed brown sugar
- 1/4 cup honey or light corn syrup
- 1/2 cup chopped pecans

Instructions:

1. **Prepare the Dough:**
   - Warm the milk in a small saucepan until it's about 110°F (45°C). Remove from heat and stir in the granulated sugar until dissolved. Sprinkle the yeast over the milk and let it sit for about 5-10 minutes, or until frothy.
   - In a large bowl, whisk together the eggs and melted butter. Add the yeast mixture and mix well.
   - Gradually add the flour and salt, stirring until a soft dough forms. Turn the dough out onto a floured surface and knead for about 5-7 minutes, until smooth and elastic.
2. **Let the Dough Rise:**
   - Place the dough in a greased bowl, cover with plastic wrap or a damp cloth, and let it rise in a warm place for about 1 hour, or until doubled in size.
3. **Prepare the Filling:**
   - In a small bowl, mix together the softened butter, brown sugar, and ground cinnamon until well combined. Set aside.
4. **Prepare the Sticky Topping:**

- In a small saucepan, melt the butter over medium heat. Stir in the brown sugar and honey (or corn syrup) until smooth. Pour this mixture into the bottom of a greased 9x13-inch baking dish. Sprinkle with chopped pecans.
5. **Assemble the Buns:**
    - Punch down the risen dough and turn it out onto a floured surface. Roll the dough into a 16x12-inch rectangle.
    - Spread the cinnamon filling evenly over the dough. Sprinkle with additional chopped pecans if desired.
    - Roll the dough tightly from the long side into a log. Slice the log into 12 equal pieces.
6. **Arrange and Bake:**
    - Place the sliced buns cut side up in the prepared baking dish over the sticky topping. Cover and let rise in a warm place for about 30 minutes.
    - Preheat your oven to 350°F (175°C).
    - Bake the buns for 25-30 minutes, or until golden brown and cooked through.
7. **Cool and Serve:**
    - Let the sticky buns cool in the pan for about 10 minutes, then invert the pan onto a serving platter so the sticky topping is on top. Serve warm.

Tips:

- **Dough Consistency:** If the dough is too sticky, add a little more flour. If too dry, add a splash of milk.
- **Rising Time:** Ensure the dough is placed in a warm, draft-free area to rise properly.
- **Topping:** Be sure to pour the sticky topping into the pan before placing the buns in so it can coat them as they bake.

Cinnamon Pecan Sticky Buns are a deliciously indulgent treat that combines sweet, spicy, and nutty flavors with a gooey caramel topping. Enjoy these buns fresh and warm for the best experience!

Cinnamon Ice Cream

Ingredients:

- 2 cups heavy cream
- 1 cup whole milk
- 3/4 cup granulated sugar
- 1/2 cup brown sugar, packed
- 1 tablespoon ground cinnamon
- 1 teaspoon vanilla extract
- 1/4 teaspoon salt
- 4 large egg yolks

Instructions:

1. **Prepare the Cinnamon Cream Mixture:**
    - In a medium saucepan, combine the heavy cream, whole milk, granulated sugar, brown sugar, ground cinnamon, and salt. Heat over medium heat, stirring occasionally, until the sugar is dissolved and the mixture is hot, but not boiling.
2. **Temper the Egg Yolks:**
    - In a separate bowl, whisk the egg yolks. Gradually add a small amount of the hot cream mixture to the egg yolks, whisking constantly to temper the eggs. This step helps to gradually raise the temperature of the egg yolks without curdling them.
3. **Cook the Custard:**
    - Pour the tempered egg yolk mixture back into the saucepan with the remaining cream mixture. Cook over medium heat, stirring constantly with a wooden spoon or silicone spatula, until the custard thickens and reaches 170-175°F (77-80°C). The custard should coat the back of the spoon.
4. **Cool the Custard:**
    - Remove the saucepan from the heat and stir in the vanilla extract. Pour the custard through a fine-mesh strainer into a clean bowl to remove any bits of cooked egg or cinnamon particles.
5. **Chill the Mixture:**
    - Let the custard cool to room temperature, then cover and refrigerate for at least 4 hours, or overnight, to chill thoroughly.
6. **Churn the Ice Cream:**
    - Once the custard is well-chilled, pour it into an ice cream maker and churn according to the manufacturer's instructions. This usually takes about 20-25 minutes.
7. **Freeze the Ice Cream:**
    - Transfer the churned ice cream to an airtight container and freeze for at least 2 hours to firm up before serving.
8. **Serve:**
    - Scoop the cinnamon ice cream into bowls or cones and enjoy!

Tips:

- **Cinnamon Stick Option:** For a more intense cinnamon flavor, you can infuse the cream mixture with a couple of cinnamon sticks. Heat the cream, milk, and sugars with the cinnamon sticks, then remove the sticks before combining with the egg yolks.
- **Egg Safety:** Make sure to cook the custard to at least 170°F (77°C) to ensure the eggs are fully cooked and safe to eat.
- **Texture:** Homemade ice cream can be softer than store-bought. Let it sit at room temperature for a few minutes before scooping if it's too hard.

Cinnamon Ice Cream is a wonderfully rich and flavorful dessert that's perfect for any occasion. Its warm, spicy notes make it a unique and comforting treat. Enjoy!

Cinnamon Banana Bread

Ingredients:

For the Banana Bread:

- 1/2 cup (1 stick) unsalted butter, softened
- 1 cup granulated sugar
- 2 large eggs
- 4 ripe bananas, mashed (about 1 1/2 cups)
- 1/4 cup milk (whole milk or 2% is best)
- 1 teaspoon vanilla extract
- 1 1/2 cups all-purpose flour
- 1 teaspoon baking powder
- 1/2 teaspoon baking soda
- 1/4 teaspoon salt

For the Cinnamon Swirl:

- 1/4 cup granulated sugar
- 1 tablespoon ground cinnamon

Instructions:

1. **Preheat the Oven:**
   - Preheat your oven to 350°F (175°C). Grease and flour a 9x5-inch loaf pan or line it with parchment paper.
2. **Prepare the Cinnamon Swirl:**
   - In a small bowl, mix together the granulated sugar and ground cinnamon. Set aside.
3. **Mix the Banana Bread Batter:**
   - In a large bowl, cream together the softened butter and granulated sugar until light and fluffy.
   - Add the eggs one at a time, beating well after each addition.
   - Stir in the mashed bananas, milk, and vanilla extract until combined.
   - In a separate bowl, whisk together the flour, baking powder, baking soda, and salt.
   - Gradually add the dry ingredients to the wet ingredients, stirring just until combined. Do not overmix.
4. **Assemble the Bread:**
   - Pour half of the batter into the prepared loaf pan.
   - Sprinkle half of the cinnamon-sugar mixture evenly over the batter.
   - Add the remaining batter on top and smooth it out.
   - Sprinkle the remaining cinnamon-sugar mixture over the top of the batter.
5. **Swirl the Cinnamon:**

- Use a knife or a skewer to gently swirl the cinnamon-sugar mixture into the batter, creating a marbled effect.
6. **Bake:**
   - Bake in the preheated oven for 60-70 minutes, or until a toothpick inserted into the center of the bread comes out clean and the top is golden brown.
7. **Cool:**
   - Allow the banana bread to cool in the pan for about 10 minutes, then transfer to a wire rack to cool completely before slicing.

Tips:

- **Ripe Bananas:** Use very ripe bananas for the best flavor and sweetness. Overripe bananas work best.
- **Mixing:** Avoid overmixing the batter; it should be just combined with some lumps.
- **Storage:** Store the cooled banana bread in an airtight container at room temperature for up to 4 days. It can also be frozen for up to 3 months. To freeze, wrap the loaf tightly in plastic wrap and foil.

Cinnamon Banana Bread is a comforting, flavorful treat that pairs wonderfully with a cup of coffee or tea. Its sweet banana flavor and spicy cinnamon swirl make it a favorite among banana bread lovers. Enjoy!

Cinnamon Swirl Cheesecake

Ingredients:

For the Crust:

- 1 1/2 cups graham cracker crumbs (about 12 whole graham crackers)
- 1/4 cup granulated sugar
- 1/2 cup unsalted butter, melted

For the Cinnamon Swirl:

- 1/4 cup granulated sugar
- 1 tablespoon ground cinnamon

For the Cheesecake Filling:

- 4 (8 oz) packages cream cheese, softened
- 1 cup granulated sugar
- 1 teaspoon vanilla extract
- 4 large eggs
- 1 cup sour cream
- 1 cup heavy cream

Instructions:

1. **Preheat the Oven:**
    - Preheat your oven to 325°F (163°C). Grease a 9-inch springform pan and line the bottom with parchment paper.
2. **Prepare the Crust:**
    - In a medium bowl, mix together the graham cracker crumbs, granulated sugar, and melted butter until well combined.
    - Press the mixture firmly into the bottom of the prepared springform pan to form an even layer.
    - Bake the crust in the preheated oven for 10 minutes. Remove from the oven and let cool while you prepare the filling.
3. **Prepare the Cinnamon Swirl:**
    - In a small bowl, mix together the granulated sugar and ground cinnamon. Set aside.
4. **Make the Cheesecake Filling:**
    - In a large bowl, beat the softened cream cheese with an electric mixer until smooth and creamy.
    - Gradually add the granulated sugar and continue to beat until well combined.
    - Beat in the vanilla extract.
    - Add the eggs one at a time, beating well after each addition.

- Mix in the sour cream and heavy cream until the batter is smooth and well combined.

5. **Assemble the Cheesecake:**
   - Pour about half of the cheesecake filling over the cooled crust in the springform pan.
   - Sprinkle about half of the cinnamon sugar mixture evenly over the batter.
   - Pour the remaining cheesecake filling over the top.
   - Use a knife or skewer to swirl the remaining cinnamon sugar mixture into the top of the cheesecake batter, creating a marble effect.

6. **Bake:**
   - Bake in the preheated oven for 55-65 minutes, or until the center is set but still slightly jiggly. The edges should be firm and the top should be lightly browned.
   - Turn off the oven and crack the oven door slightly. Let the cheesecake cool in the oven for 1 hour to prevent cracking.

7. **Chill:**
   - After cooling, cover the cheesecake and refrigerate for at least 4 hours or overnight to fully set.

8. **Serve:**
   - Run a knife around the edge of the cheesecake to loosen it from the pan. Remove the sides of the springform pan.
   - Slice and serve chilled.

Tips:

- **Cream Cheese:** Make sure the cream cheese is fully softened to avoid lumps in the batter.
- **Swirling:** Don't over-swirl the cinnamon mixture; you want to create a marbled effect without completely mixing it into the batter.
- **Prevent Cracking:** Cooling the cheesecake slowly in the oven with the door slightly open helps prevent cracks.

Cinnamon Swirl Cheesecake is a wonderful dessert that combines the creamy richness of cheesecake with a hint of warm, comforting cinnamon. Enjoy this delightful treat with a dollop of whipped cream or a sprinkle of extra cinnamon sugar!

Cinnamon-Spiced Sweet Potatoes

Ingredients:

- 4 medium sweet potatoes (about 2 lbs), peeled and cut into 1-inch cubes
- 2 tablespoons olive oil or melted butter
- 1/4 cup brown sugar, packed
- 1 teaspoon ground cinnamon
- 1/2 teaspoon ground nutmeg
- 1/4 teaspoon ground ginger (optional)
- 1/4 teaspoon salt
- 1/4 teaspoon black pepper
- 1/4 cup chopped pecans or walnuts (optional, for garnish)
- 1 tablespoon honey or maple syrup (optional, for drizzling)

Instructions:

1. **Preheat the Oven:**
    - Preheat your oven to 400°F (200°C). Line a baking sheet with parchment paper or lightly grease it.
2. **Prepare the Sweet Potatoes:**
    - Place the cubed sweet potatoes in a large bowl. Drizzle with olive oil or melted butter and toss to coat.
3. **Season the Sweet Potatoes:**
    - In a small bowl, mix together the brown sugar, ground cinnamon, ground nutmeg, ground ginger (if using), salt, and black pepper.
    - Sprinkle the spice mixture over the sweet potatoes and toss until the cubes are evenly coated.
4. **Roast the Sweet Potatoes:**
    - Spread the seasoned sweet potatoes in a single layer on the prepared baking sheet.
    - Roast in the preheated oven for 25-30 minutes, or until the sweet potatoes are tender and caramelized. Toss halfway through the cooking time to ensure even roasting.
5. **Add Optional Garnishes:**
    - If desired, sprinkle chopped pecans or walnuts over the sweet potatoes during the last 5 minutes of roasting for added crunch and flavor.
    - Drizzle with honey or maple syrup before serving for extra sweetness.
6. **Serve:**
    - Transfer the roasted sweet potatoes to a serving dish and enjoy warm.

Tips:

- **Cut Size:** Ensure the sweet potato cubes are of uniform size to promote even cooking.

- **Even Coating:** Toss the sweet potatoes thoroughly with the oil and seasoning to ensure even flavor distribution.
- **Storage:** Store leftovers in an airtight container in the refrigerator for up to 4 days. Reheat in the oven or microwave before serving.

Cinnamon-Spiced Sweet Potatoes are a flavorful and versatile side dish that pairs well with a variety of main courses. Their sweet and spicy profile makes them a favorite for both everyday meals and special occasions. Enjoy!

Cinnamon Almond Granola Bars

Ingredients:

- 2 cups old-fashioned rolled oats
- 1 cup chopped almonds (or other nuts of your choice)
- 1/2 cup honey or maple syrup
- 1/2 cup almond butter (or peanut butter)
- 1/4 cup brown sugar, packed
- 1 teaspoon ground cinnamon
- 1/4 teaspoon salt
- 1/2 cup mini chocolate chips or dried fruit (optional, for added sweetness or texture)

Instructions:

1. **Preheat the Oven:**
   - Preheat your oven to 350°F (175°C). Line an 8x8-inch baking dish with parchment paper, leaving an overhang on the sides for easy removal.
2. **Toast the Oats and Nuts:**
   - Spread the rolled oats and chopped almonds evenly on a baking sheet. Toast in the preheated oven for about 10 minutes, or until golden and fragrant. Stir halfway through to ensure even toasting. Remove from the oven and let cool slightly.
3. **Prepare the Binding Mixture:**
   - In a medium saucepan, combine the honey (or maple syrup), almond butter, brown sugar, ground cinnamon, and salt. Heat over medium heat, stirring frequently, until the mixture is smooth and the sugar has dissolved, about 3-4 minutes.
4. **Mix Ingredients:**
   - In a large bowl, combine the toasted oats and almonds. Pour the warm honey mixture over the oats and almonds, and stir well to coat evenly.
5. **Add Optional Ingredients:**
   - If using, fold in the mini chocolate chips or dried fruit at this stage.
6. **Press into the Pan:**
   - Transfer the mixture to the prepared baking dish. Press it down firmly and evenly with the back of a spatula or the bottom of a glass to ensure the bars hold together well.
7. **Cool and Cut:**
   - Allow the granola bars to cool completely in the pan, at room temperature or in the refrigerator for faster cooling. Once cooled and set, lift the bars out of the pan using the parchment paper overhang and cut into squares or rectangles.
8. **Store:**
   - Store the granola bars in an airtight container at room temperature for up to 1 week, or in the refrigerator for up to 2 weeks. They can also be frozen for up to 3 months.

Tips:

- **Consistency:** Make sure to press the mixture firmly into the pan to ensure the bars stick together.
- **Nut Alternatives:** Feel free to substitute or mix in other nuts or seeds according to your preference.
- **Sweetness:** Adjust the amount of honey or maple syrup based on your desired level of sweetness.

Cinnamon Almond Granola Bars are a tasty, wholesome snack that's easy to make and perfect for busy days. Enjoy them as a quick breakfast, a post-workout snack, or an afternoon treat!

Cinnamon Hot Chocolate

Ingredients:

- 2 cups whole milk (or any milk of your choice)
- 1/2 cup heavy cream
- 1/2 cup semi-sweet chocolate chips or chopped chocolate
- 1/4 cup cocoa powder
- 1/4 cup granulated sugar (adjust to taste)
- 1/2 teaspoon ground cinnamon
- 1/4 teaspoon vanilla extract
- Pinch of salt
- Whipped cream (optional, for topping)
- Additional cinnamon sticks or ground cinnamon (optional, for garnish)

Instructions:

1. **Heat the Milk and Cream:**
   - In a medium saucepan, combine the milk and heavy cream. Heat over medium heat until the mixture is hot but not boiling, stirring occasionally.
2. **Mix Cocoa and Sugar:**
   - In a separate bowl, whisk together the cocoa powder, granulated sugar, and ground cinnamon.
3. **Add Chocolate:**
   - Once the milk mixture is hot, add the chocolate chips or chopped chocolate. Stir until the chocolate is completely melted and the mixture is smooth.
4. **Combine Cocoa Mixture:**
   - Gradually whisk in the cocoa powder and sugar mixture into the hot chocolate mixture. Continue to stir until well combined and smooth.
5. **Flavor and Adjust:**
   - Stir in the vanilla extract and a pinch of salt. Taste and adjust sweetness or cinnamon according to your preference.
6. **Serve:**
   - Pour the hot chocolate into mugs. Top with whipped cream and a sprinkle of ground cinnamon or a cinnamon stick if desired.
7. **Garnish:**
   - For extra flavor, you can garnish with additional cinnamon sticks or a dash of ground cinnamon.

Tips:

- **Chocolate Choice:** Use high-quality chocolate chips or chopped chocolate for the best flavor. Dark chocolate can be used for a richer taste.
- **Sweetness:** Adjust the sugar according to your taste preference. You can also use alternative sweeteners like honey or maple syrup.

- **Creaminess:** For a richer hot chocolate, you can increase the amount of heavy cream or use half-and-half instead of milk.

Cinnamon Hot Chocolate is a delightful and indulgent treat that warms you from the inside out. Enjoy it by the fireplace or as a sweet ending to your day!

Cinnamon Roll Cheesecake

Ingredients:

For the Crust:

- 1 1/2 cups graham cracker crumbs
- 1/4 cup granulated sugar
- 1/2 cup unsalted butter, melted

For the Cinnamon Swirl:

- 1/4 cup granulated sugar
- 1 tablespoon ground cinnamon
- 2 tablespoons unsalted butter, melted

For the Cheesecake Filling:

- 4 (8 oz) packages cream cheese, softened
- 1 cup granulated sugar
- 1 teaspoon vanilla extract
- 4 large eggs
- 1 cup sour cream
- 1 cup heavy cream

For the Cream Cheese Frosting (Optional):

- 4 oz cream cheese, softened
- 2 tablespoons unsalted butter, softened
- 1 cup powdered sugar
- 1/2 teaspoon vanilla extract
- 1-2 tablespoons milk (as needed for consistency)

Instructions:

1. **Preheat the Oven:**
    - Preheat your oven to 325°F (163°C). Grease a 9-inch springform pan and line the bottom with parchment paper.
2. **Prepare the Crust:**
    - In a medium bowl, mix together the graham cracker crumbs, granulated sugar, and melted butter until well combined.
    - Press the mixture firmly into the bottom of the prepared springform pan to form an even layer.
    - Bake the crust in the preheated oven for 10 minutes. Remove from the oven and let cool while you prepare the filling.
3. **Prepare the Cinnamon Swirl:**

- In a small bowl, mix together the granulated sugar, ground cinnamon, and melted butter until well combined. Set aside.

4. **Make the Cheesecake Filling:**
   - In a large bowl, beat the softened cream cheese with an electric mixer until smooth and creamy.
   - Gradually add the granulated sugar and beat until well combined.
   - Beat in the vanilla extract.
   - Add the eggs one at a time, beating well after each addition.
   - Mix in the sour cream and heavy cream until the batter is smooth and well combined.

5. **Assemble the Cheesecake:**
   - Pour about half of the cheesecake filling over the cooled crust in the springform pan.
   - Spoon dollops of the cinnamon swirl mixture over the filling.
   - Pour the remaining cheesecake filling over the top.
   - Use a knife or skewer to swirl the cinnamon mixture into the top of the cheesecake batter, creating a marble effect.

6. **Bake:**
   - Bake in the preheated oven for 55-65 minutes, or until the center is set but still slightly jiggly. The edges should be firm and the top should be lightly browned.
   - Turn off the oven and crack the oven door slightly. Let the cheesecake cool in the oven for 1 hour to prevent cracking.

7. **Chill:**
   - After cooling, cover the cheesecake and refrigerate for at least 4 hours or overnight to fully set.

8. **Prepare the Cream Cheese Frosting (Optional):**
   - In a medium bowl, beat together the softened cream cheese and butter until smooth.
   - Gradually add the powdered sugar, beating until well combined.
   - Stir in the vanilla extract.
   - Add milk as needed to achieve a spreadable consistency.

9. **Serve:**
   - Run a knife around the edge of the cheesecake to loosen it from the pan. Remove the sides of the springform pan.
   - Spread the cream cheese frosting over the top of the chilled cheesecake, if desired.
   - Slice and serve.

Tips:

- **Cream Cheese:** Ensure the cream cheese is fully softened to avoid lumps in the batter.
- **Swirling:** Don't over-swirl the cinnamon mixture; you want to create a marbled effect without completely mixing it into the batter.

- **Cracking:** Cooling the cheesecake slowly in the oven with the door slightly open helps prevent cracks.

Cinnamon Roll Cheesecake is a luxurious dessert that combines two beloved treats into one irresistible indulgence. Enjoy every creamy, spiced bite!

Cinnamon Apple Scones

Ingredients:

For the Scones:

- 2 1/2 cups all-purpose flour
- 1/3 cup granulated sugar
- 1 tablespoon baking powder
- 1/2 teaspoon salt
- 1/2 cup cold unsalted butter, cut into small pieces
- 1 cup peeled and diced apples (about 1 medium apple)
- 1 teaspoon ground cinnamon
- 1/2 teaspoon ground nutmeg
- 1/2 cup milk (whole or 2%)
- 1 large egg
- 1 teaspoon vanilla extract

For the Cinnamon Sugar Topping (Optional):

- 2 tablespoons granulated sugar
- 1 teaspoon ground cinnamon

Instructions:

1. **Preheat the Oven:**
   - Preheat your oven to 400°F (200°C). Line a baking sheet with parchment paper or lightly grease it.
2. **Prepare the Dry Ingredients:**
   - In a large bowl, whisk together the flour, granulated sugar, baking powder, and salt.
3. **Cut in the Butter:**
   - Add the cold, cubed butter to the flour mixture. Use a pastry cutter or your fingers to work the butter into the flour until the mixture resembles coarse crumbs.
4. **Prepare the Apples:**
   - In a small bowl, toss the diced apples with 1 teaspoon of ground cinnamon and 1/2 teaspoon of ground nutmeg.
5. **Mix the Wet Ingredients:**
   - In another bowl, whisk together the milk, egg, and vanilla extract.
6. **Combine Ingredients:**
   - Add the milk mixture to the flour mixture and stir until just combined. Gently fold in the spiced apples.
7. **Shape the Scones:**
   - Turn the dough out onto a floured surface and gently knead it a few times until it comes together. Pat the dough into a 1-inch thick circle.

- Use a sharp knife or a pizza cutter to cut the dough into 8 wedges.
8. **Add the Topping (Optional):**
    - In a small bowl, mix together the granulated sugar and ground cinnamon. Sprinkle this mixture evenly over the top of the scones.
9. **Bake:**
    - Transfer the scones to the prepared baking sheet, spacing them about 2 inches apart.
    - Bake in the preheated oven for 15-18 minutes, or until the scones are golden brown and a toothpick inserted into the center comes out clean.
10. **Cool:**
    - Allow the scones to cool on the baking sheet for a few minutes before transferring them to a wire rack to cool completely.

Tips:

- **Butter:** Ensure the butter is very cold for the best texture in the scones.
- **Apples:** Use a firm, crisp apple like Honeycrisp or Granny Smith for the best results.
- **Mixing:** Avoid over-mixing the dough; it should be slightly lumpy to ensure tender scones.

Cinnamon Apple Scones are a delightful combination of flaky, buttery scones with the warm flavors of cinnamon and apple. Enjoy them fresh from the oven with a cup of tea or coffee!

Cinnamon and Honey Butter

Ingredients:

- 1/2 cup unsalted butter, softened
- 1/4 cup honey
- 1/4 cup powdered sugar
- 1 teaspoon ground cinnamon
- 1/4 teaspoon vanilla extract (optional)

Instructions:

1. **Soften the Butter:**
    - Make sure the butter is softened to room temperature for easy mixing. If you forgot to take it out in advance, you can microwave it in 10-second intervals until soft, but be careful not to melt it.
2. **Mix Ingredients:**
    - In a medium bowl, combine the softened butter, honey, powdered sugar, and ground cinnamon. If using, add the vanilla extract.
3. **Beat Until Smooth:**
    - Using a hand mixer or a stand mixer fitted with the paddle attachment, beat the mixture on medium speed until smooth and creamy. Scrape down the sides of the bowl as needed to ensure everything is well combined.
4. **Taste and Adjust:**
    - Taste the butter and adjust the sweetness or cinnamon according to your preference. Add more honey or cinnamon if desired.
5. **Serve:**
    - Transfer the cinnamon and honey butter to a serving dish or an airtight container.
6. **Store:**
    - Store in the refrigerator for up to 2 weeks. Let it come to room temperature before serving to make it easier to spread.

Tips:

- **Butter Consistency:** Ensure the butter is soft but not melted to achieve the best texture.
- **Honey:** Use a high-quality honey for the best flavor.
- **Serving:** This butter is great on toast, biscuits, pancakes, waffles, or even as a sweetener for oatmeal or yogurt.

Cinnamon and Honey Butter adds a touch of sweetness and warmth to any bread or breakfast item, making it a delightful treat that's easy to prepare and enjoy!

Cinnamon Flavored Syrup

Ingredients:

- 1 cup granulated sugar
- 1 cup water
- 1 tablespoon ground cinnamon
- 1 teaspoon vanilla extract (optional)
- 1 tablespoon light corn syrup or maple syrup (optional, for added richness)

Instructions:

1. **Combine Ingredients:**
   - In a medium saucepan, combine the granulated sugar, water, and ground cinnamon.
2. **Heat the Syrup:**
   - Place the saucepan over medium heat. Stir continuously until the sugar is fully dissolved and the mixture starts to simmer. Do not let it boil vigorously.
3. **Simmer:**
   - Once the sugar is dissolved, reduce the heat to low and let the syrup simmer for about 5-10 minutes. This allows the cinnamon flavor to infuse into the syrup and the mixture to thicken slightly.
4. **Add Optional Ingredients:**
   - If desired, stir in the vanilla extract and light corn syrup or maple syrup for added flavor and richness.
5. **Cool and Store:**
   - Remove the saucepan from heat and let the syrup cool slightly. It will thicken a bit more as it cools.
   - Transfer the syrup to a clean jar or bottle. Store in the refrigerator for up to 2 weeks.
6. **Serve:**
   - Reheat gently before serving if needed. Pour over pancakes, waffles, french toast, or use as a sweetener in beverages.

Tips:

- **Thickening:** If you prefer a thicker syrup, simmer it a bit longer. Keep in mind it will thicken further as it cools.
- **Spice Level:** Adjust the amount of ground cinnamon based on your preference. You can also use cinnamon sticks instead of ground cinnamon for a more subtle flavor; just remove the sticks before serving.
- **Flavor Variations:** Feel free to experiment with other spices like nutmeg or allspice for a different flavor profile.

Cinnamon Flavored Syrup is a versatile and delicious addition to your breakfast repertoire, bringing a touch of warmth and sweetness to your morning meals!

Cinnamon Spiced Rice Pudding

Ingredients:

- 1 cup Arborio rice (short-grain rice)
- 4 cups whole milk
- 1/2 cup granulated sugar
- 1/4 cup brown sugar, packed
- 1/4 teaspoon salt
- 1 teaspoon ground cinnamon
- 1/4 teaspoon ground nutmeg
- 1/2 teaspoon vanilla extract
- 1/2 cup raisins or sultanas (optional)
- Ground cinnamon and sugar for garnish (optional)

Instructions:

1. **Rinse the Rice:**
   - Rinse the Arborio rice under cold water until the water runs clear. This helps remove excess starch and prevents the pudding from becoming overly thick.
2. **Cook the Rice:**
   - In a large saucepan, combine the rinsed rice and 1 cup of milk. Bring to a boil over medium-high heat, stirring frequently.
3. **Simmer:**
   - Once the milk starts to boil, reduce the heat to low. Cover and simmer for about 10-15 minutes, stirring occasionally, until the rice is partially cooked and the milk is absorbed.
4. **Add Remaining Ingredients:**
   - Stir in the remaining 3 cups of milk, granulated sugar, brown sugar, salt, ground cinnamon, and ground nutmeg. Continue to cook over low heat, stirring frequently, until the rice is fully cooked and the mixture has thickened to a creamy consistency, about 20-25 minutes.
5. **Add Raisins (Optional):**
   - If using raisins, stir them into the pudding during the last 5 minutes of cooking.
6. **Finish and Flavor:**
   - Remove the saucepan from heat and stir in the vanilla extract. Taste and adjust the sweetness or spice level if needed.
7. **Cool:**
   - Allow the rice pudding to cool slightly before serving. It can be enjoyed warm or chilled.
8. **Serve:**
   - Spoon the rice pudding into serving bowls. Garnish with a sprinkle of ground cinnamon and a bit of sugar if desired.

Tips:

- **Creaminess:** For extra creaminess, you can substitute some of the milk with half-and-half or heavy cream.
- **Consistency:** The pudding will thicken as it cools. If it becomes too thick, stir in a little more milk to reach your desired consistency.
- **Flavor Variations:** Feel free to add other spices like cardamom or cloves for additional flavor.

Cinnamon Spiced Rice Pudding is a comforting and satisfying dessert that's sure to please. Its creamy texture and warm spices make it a perfect choice for a cozy treat!

Cinnamon Swirl Cake

Ingredients:

For the Cake:

- 1 1/2 cups all-purpose flour
- 1 cup granulated sugar
- 1/2 cup unsalted butter, softened
- 2 large eggs
- 1 cup sour cream
- 1/2 cup milk
- 1 1/2 teaspoons baking powder
- 1/2 teaspoon baking soda
- 1/4 teaspoon salt
- 1 teaspoon vanilla extract

For the Cinnamon Swirl:

- 1/2 cup granulated sugar
- 1 tablespoon ground cinnamon
- 2 tablespoons unsalted butter, melted

For the Glaze (Optional):

- 1 cup powdered sugar
- 2 tablespoons milk
- 1/2 teaspoon vanilla extract

Instructions:

1. **Preheat the Oven:**
   - Preheat your oven to 350°F (175°C). Grease and flour a 9-inch round cake pan or a 9x9-inch square baking pan.
2. **Prepare the Cinnamon Swirl:**
   - In a small bowl, mix together the granulated sugar, ground cinnamon, and melted butter. Set aside.
3. **Make the Cake Batter:**
   - In a large bowl, beat the softened butter and granulated sugar together until light and fluffy.
   - Add the eggs one at a time, beating well after each addition.
   - Mix in the vanilla extract.
   - In a separate bowl, whisk together the flour, baking powder, baking soda, and salt.

- Gradually add the dry ingredients to the butter mixture, alternating with the sour cream and milk, beginning and ending with the dry ingredients. Mix until just combined.

4. **Assemble the Cake:**
    - Spread half of the cake batter evenly in the prepared pan.
    - Sprinkle half of the cinnamon swirl mixture over the batter.
    - Spread the remaining batter over the cinnamon swirl layer.
    - Sprinkle the remaining cinnamon swirl mixture on top of the batter. Use a knife or a toothpick to gently swirl the cinnamon mixture into the batter, creating a marbled effect.

5. **Bake:**
    - Bake in the preheated oven for 30-35 minutes, or until a toothpick inserted into the center of the cake comes out clean.
    - Let the cake cool in the pan for 10 minutes before transferring it to a wire rack to cool completely.

6. **Prepare the Glaze (Optional):**
    - In a small bowl, whisk together the powdered sugar, milk, and vanilla extract until smooth. Drizzle over the cooled cake.

7. **Serve:**
    - Once the glaze has set, slice and serve the cake.

Tips:

- **Butter:** Ensure the butter is softened for easier mixing and a smoother batter.
- **Swirling:** Be gentle when swirling the cinnamon mixture to avoid mixing it too much into the batter.
- **Glaze:** The glaze is optional but adds a sweet finishing touch to the cake.

Cinnamon Swirl Cake is a comforting and flavorful treat with a beautiful swirl of cinnamon in every bite. Enjoy it with a cup of coffee or tea for a perfect pairing!

Cinnamon Raisin Overnight Oats

Ingredients:

- 1 cup rolled oats
- 1 cup milk (any kind: dairy, almond, soy, etc.)
- 1/2 cup Greek yogurt (plain or vanilla)
- 1 tablespoon chia seeds (optional, for added texture and nutrition)
- 2 tablespoons honey or maple syrup (adjust to taste)
- 1 teaspoon ground cinnamon
- 1/4 teaspoon vanilla extract
- 1/4 cup raisins
- Fresh fruit or nuts for topping (optional)

Instructions:

1. **Combine Ingredients:**
   - In a medium bowl or a mason jar, combine the rolled oats, milk, Greek yogurt, chia seeds (if using), honey or maple syrup, ground cinnamon, and vanilla extract.
2. **Stir in Raisins:**
   - Mix in the raisins, ensuring they are evenly distributed throughout the oat mixture.
3. **Refrigerate:**
   - Cover the bowl or jar with a lid or plastic wrap. Refrigerate overnight, or for at least 4-6 hours, to allow the oats to absorb the liquid and soften.
4. **Serve:**
   - In the morning, give the oats a good stir. If the mixture is too thick, you can add a little more milk to reach your desired consistency.
5. **Top and Enjoy:**
   - Top with fresh fruit, nuts, or additional raisins if desired. Enjoy your healthy and flavorful breakfast!

Tips:

- **Sweetness:** Adjust the sweetness by adding more honey or maple syrup if you like it sweeter.
- **Chia Seeds:** Adding chia seeds not only enhances the texture but also boosts the nutritional value of your overnight oats.
- **Texture:** If you prefer a creamier texture, you can use a bit more yogurt or milk. For a thicker consistency, reduce the amount of milk.

Cinnamon Raisin Overnight Oats are a convenient and tasty breakfast that can be customized with your favorite add-ins and toppings. Enjoy this nutritious start to your day!

Cinnamon and Nutmeg Pancakes

Ingredients:

- 1 1/2 cups all-purpose flour
- 2 tablespoons granulated sugar
- 1 tablespoon baking powder
- 1/2 teaspoon salt
- 1 teaspoon ground cinnamon
- 1/4 teaspoon ground nutmeg
- 1 large egg
- 1 1/4 cups milk (whole, 2%, or a dairy-free alternative)
- 1/4 cup unsalted butter, melted (plus more for cooking)
- 1 teaspoon vanilla extract

Instructions:

1. **Preheat the Pan:**
    - Heat a non-stick skillet or griddle over medium heat. Lightly grease with a small amount of butter or oil.
2. **Mix Dry Ingredients:**
    - In a large bowl, whisk together the flour, granulated sugar, baking powder, salt, ground cinnamon, and ground nutmeg.
3. **Prepare Wet Ingredients:**
    - In a separate bowl, beat the egg and then mix in the milk, melted butter, and vanilla extract.
4. **Combine Ingredients:**
    - Pour the wet ingredients into the dry ingredients. Stir until just combined. The batter will be a bit lumpy, which is fine—over-mixing can lead to tough pancakes.
5. **Cook the Pancakes:**
    - Pour about 1/4 cup of batter onto the preheated skillet for each pancake. Cook until bubbles form on the surface and the edges look set, about 2-3 minutes. Flip the pancake and cook until golden brown on the other side, about 1-2 more minutes.
6. **Serve:**
    - Transfer the pancakes to a plate and keep warm while you cook the remaining pancakes. Serve with maple syrup, fresh fruit, or your favorite toppings.

Tips:

- **Consistency:** If the batter is too thick, add a little more milk to reach your desired consistency. If too thin, add a bit more flour.
- **Keep Warm:** To keep pancakes warm while cooking the rest, place them on a baking sheet in a low oven (about 200°F or 95°C).
- **Flavor Variations:** You can add a handful of chocolate chips, nuts, or fresh fruit to the batter for extra flavor and texture.

Cinnamon and Nutmeg Pancakes are a wonderful way to start the day with a burst of warm, comforting spices. Enjoy them with your favorite breakfast accompaniments!

Cinnamon Apple Smoothie

Ingredients:

- 1 medium apple, peeled, cored, and chopped (any variety you like, such as Fuji, Gala, or Granny Smith)
- 1/2 cup Greek yogurt (plain or vanilla)
- 1/2 cup milk (dairy or non-dairy, such as almond or oat milk)
- 1/2 cup ice cubes
- 1 tablespoon honey or maple syrup (optional, for added sweetness)
- 1/2 teaspoon ground cinnamon
- 1/4 teaspoon vanilla extract (optional)
- A pinch of nutmeg (optional, for extra spice)

Instructions:

1. **Prepare the Ingredients:**
   - Chop the apple into small pieces. If you prefer a smoother texture, you can peel the apple, but leaving the skin on adds extra fiber and nutrients.
2. **Blend the Smoothie:**
   - In a blender, combine the chopped apple, Greek yogurt, milk, ice cubes, honey or maple syrup (if using), ground cinnamon, and vanilla extract (if using).
3. **Blend Until Smooth:**
   - Blend on high speed until the mixture is smooth and creamy. If the smoothie is too thick, add a little more milk to reach your desired consistency. If it's too thin, add a few more ice cubes or a small handful of oats for thickness.
4. **Taste and Adjust:**
   - Taste the smoothie and adjust the sweetness or spice level as needed. You can add more honey, cinnamon, or a pinch of nutmeg if desired.
5. **Serve:**
   - Pour the smoothie into a glass and enjoy immediately. You can also refrigerate it for a short while if you prefer it chilled.

Tips:

- **Apple Variety:** Choose a sweet variety of apple for a naturally sweeter smoothie. Granny Smith apples are tart but add a nice contrast to the sweetness of the yogurt and honey.
- **Texture:** For a creamier smoothie, use a higher-fat yogurt or add a tablespoon of nut butter.
- **Toppings:** Garnish with a sprinkle of cinnamon on top, or add some granola for a crunchy texture.

Cinnamon Apple Smoothie is a delicious and easy way to enjoy the flavors of apple pie in a healthy, drinkable form. Enjoy it as a part of your morning routine or as a refreshing snack!

Cinnamon Caramel Sauce

Ingredients:

- 1 cup granulated sugar
- 6 tablespoons unsalted butter, cut into pieces
- 1/2 cup heavy cream
- 1 teaspoon ground cinnamon
- 1/4 teaspoon salt
- 1/2 teaspoon vanilla extract (optional)

Instructions:

1. **Prepare the Ingredients:**
   - Measure out all the ingredients before you start, as the caramel-making process moves quickly.
2. **Cook the Sugar:**
   - In a medium saucepan over medium heat, melt the granulated sugar. Stir constantly with a heat-resistant spatula or wooden spoon to ensure even melting and to prevent burning.
3. **Caramelize the Sugar:**
   - Continue stirring until the sugar is fully melted and turns a deep amber color. This process usually takes about 5-7 minutes. Be careful not to let it burn; the sugar should have a rich golden-brown color.
4. **Add the Butter:**
   - Once the sugar is fully melted and amber-colored, carefully add the pieces of butter to the pan. The mixture will bubble vigorously, so be cautious.
5. **Stir in the Cream:**
   - After the butter is melted and fully incorporated into the sugar, slowly pour in the heavy cream while stirring continuously. The mixture will bubble up again, so stir gently.
6. **Add Cinnamon and Salt:**
   - Stir in the ground cinnamon and salt. If you're using vanilla extract, add it now and stir to combine.
7. **Simmer:**
   - Let the sauce simmer for another 1-2 minutes, stirring constantly, until it reaches your desired thickness. The sauce will thicken as it cools.
8. **Cool and Store:**
   - Remove the saucepan from heat and let the sauce cool slightly before transferring it to a heatproof jar or container. The sauce can be stored in the refrigerator for up to 2 weeks. Reheat gently before using, if needed.

Tips:

- **Consistency:** If the sauce is too thick after cooling, you can reheat it gently and stir in a bit more cream to reach your desired consistency.
- **Flavor Adjustments:** Feel free to adjust the amount of cinnamon according to your taste. You can also experiment with other spices like nutmeg or cardamom for a unique twist.

- **Safety:** Be cautious when working with hot caramel. It can cause burns if it comes into contact with your skin.

Cinnamon Caramel Sauce is a rich, flavorful addition to many desserts and breakfast items, offering a sweet and spicy kick that enhances any dish it accompanies. Enjoy it drizzled over your favorite treats!

Cinnamon Sugar Shortbread Cookies

Ingredients:

- 1 cup unsalted butter, softened

- 1/2 cup granulated sugar
- 1/2 teaspoon vanilla extract
- 2 cups all-purpose flour
- 1/2 teaspoon salt
- 1 tablespoon ground cinnamon
- 1/4 cup additional granulated sugar (for rolling)

Instructions:

1. **Preheat the Oven:**
   - Preheat your oven to 350°F (175°C). Line a baking sheet with parchment paper or a silicone baking mat.
2. **Cream Butter and Sugar:**
   - In a large bowl, beat the softened butter and 1/2 cup granulated sugar together until light and fluffy, using an electric mixer on medium speed.
3. **Add Vanilla:**
   - Mix in the vanilla extract until well combined.
4. **Combine Dry Ingredients:**
   - In a separate bowl, whisk together the flour, salt, and ground cinnamon.
5. **Mix Dry and Wet Ingredients:**
   - Gradually add the dry ingredients to the butter mixture, mixing on low speed until the dough just comes together. Avoid overmixing.
6. **Shape the Cookies:**
   - Roll the dough into 1-inch balls and place them on the prepared baking sheet. Flatten each ball slightly with the bottom of a glass or your fingers.
7. **Coat with Cinnamon Sugar:**
   - In a small bowl, combine the additional 1/4 cup granulated sugar with a pinch of ground cinnamon. Roll each flattened dough ball in the cinnamon sugar mixture, then place it back on the baking sheet.
8. **Bake:**
   - Bake in the preheated oven for 12-15 minutes, or until the edges of the cookies are lightly golden. The centers should still be pale.
9. **Cool:**
   - Allow the cookies to cool on the baking sheet for a few minutes before transferring them to a wire rack to cool completely.

Tips:

- **Butter:** Make sure the butter is softened to room temperature for easy mixing and a smooth dough.
- **Texture:** Don't overmix the dough to ensure your cookies remain tender and crumbly.
- **Variations:** You can add a bit of finely chopped nuts or a drizzle of icing if you like.

Cinnamon Sugar Shortbread Cookies are a classic treat with a delightful balance of buttery richness and warm cinnamon flavor. Enjoy them with a cup of tea or coffee!

Cinnamon Maple Bacon

Ingredients:

- 1 pound (450 g) thick-cut bacon
- 1/2 cup pure maple syrup

- 1/4 cup brown sugar, packed
- 1 teaspoon ground cinnamon
- 1/4 teaspoon ground nutmeg (optional)
- 1/4 teaspoon salt (optional)

Instructions:

1. **Preheat the Oven:**
   - Preheat your oven to 375°F (190°C). Line a baking sheet with aluminum foil or parchment paper for easy cleanup. Place a wire rack on top of the baking sheet if you have one; this helps the bacon cook evenly and become crispier.
2. **Prepare the Glaze:**
   - In a small bowl, combine the maple syrup, brown sugar, ground cinnamon, and ground nutmeg (if using). Stir until the brown sugar is fully dissolved and the mixture is well combined.
3. **Arrange the Bacon:**
   - Arrange the bacon slices in a single layer on the wire rack or directly on the lined baking sheet. You can overlap them slightly if needed, but try to keep them as flat as possible for even cooking.
4. **Apply the Glaze:**
   - Brush the bacon slices with the cinnamon maple glaze, making sure to coat them evenly. Reserve some of the glaze for brushing during baking.
5. **Bake the Bacon:**
   - Bake in the preheated oven for 15-20 minutes, or until the bacon is crispy and caramelized. Keep an eye on it towards the end of the baking time to prevent burning. Brush the bacon with the remaining glaze halfway through the cooking time for extra flavor.
6. **Cool and Serve:**
   - Remove the bacon from the oven and let it cool on the wire rack for a few minutes. The bacon will continue to crisp up as it cools.
7. **Serve:**
   - Enjoy the Cinnamon Maple Bacon warm as a delicious addition to breakfast, brunch, or as a unique snack. It pairs well with eggs, pancakes, or even crumbled over salads.

Tips:

- **Bacon Thickness:** Thick-cut bacon works best for this recipe as it holds up well during baking and allows the glaze to caramelize nicely.
- **Glaze Application:** Be careful not to apply too much glaze, as it can cause the bacon to burn if it pools.
- **Storage:** Store leftover bacon in an airtight container in the refrigerator for up to a week. Reheat in the oven to retain crispiness.

Cinnamon Maple Bacon offers a wonderful combination of sweet and savory flavors, making it a standout addition to any meal. Enjoy its unique taste and aroma!

Cinnamon Swirled Cupcakes

Ingredients:

For the Cupcakes:

- 1 1/2 cups all-purpose flour
- 1 cup granulated sugar
- 1 1/2 teaspoons baking powder
- 1/4 teaspoon salt
- 1/2 cup unsalted butter, softened
- 2 large eggs
- 1/2 cup milk (dairy or non-dairy)
- 1 teaspoon vanilla extract
- 1/2 teaspoon ground cinnamon

For the Cinnamon Swirl:

- 1/4 cup granulated sugar
- 1 tablespoon ground cinnamon
- 2 tablespoons unsalted butter, melted

For the Frosting (Optional):

- 1/2 cup unsalted butter, softened
- 1 1/2 cups powdered sugar
- 1/4 cup milk
- 1/2 teaspoon vanilla extract
- 1/2 teaspoon ground cinnamon

Instructions:

1. **Preheat the Oven:**
   - Preheat your oven to 350°F (175°C). Line a muffin tin with cupcake liners.
2. **Prepare the Cinnamon Swirl:**
   - In a small bowl, mix together the granulated sugar, ground cinnamon, and melted butter until well combined. Set aside.
3. **Mix Dry Ingredients:**
   - In a medium bowl, whisk together the flour, baking powder, salt, and ground cinnamon.
4. **Cream Butter and Sugar:**
   - In a large bowl, beat the softened butter and granulated sugar together until light and fluffy.
5. **Add Eggs and Vanilla:**
   - Beat in the eggs one at a time, mixing well after each addition. Stir in the vanilla extract.
6. **Combine Ingredients:**
   - Gradually add the dry ingredients to the butter mixture, alternating with the milk, beginning and ending with the dry ingredients. Mix until just combined.
7. **Add Cinnamon Swirl:**

        - Spoon a small amount of cupcake batter into each cupcake liner, followed by a spoonful of the cinnamon swirl mixture. Top with another spoonful of batter, and use a toothpick or skewer to gently swirl the cinnamon mixture into the batter.
8. **Bake:**
    - Bake in the preheated oven for 18-20 minutes, or until a toothpick inserted into the center of a cupcake comes out clean. Allow cupcakes to cool in the pan for a few minutes before transferring them to a wire rack to cool completely.
9. **Prepare the Frosting (Optional):**
    - In a medium bowl, beat the softened butter until creamy. Gradually add the powdered sugar, milk, vanilla extract, and ground cinnamon. Beat until smooth and fluffy.
10. **Frost and Serve:**
    - Once the cupcakes are completely cooled, frost them with the cinnamon frosting if desired.

Tips:

- **Swirling:** Be gentle when swirling the cinnamon mixture to ensure it's evenly distributed without mixing too much into the batter.
- **Frosting:** If you prefer, you can skip the frosting and simply sprinkle the cooled cupcakes with powdered sugar for a lighter touch.
- **Storage:** Store cupcakes in an airtight container at room temperature for up to 3 days, or refrigerate for up to a week.

Cinnamon Swirled Cupcakes offer a delightful blend of cinnamon sweetness and fluffy cake texture, making them a perfect treat for any time you want something a bit special. Enjoy!

Cinnamon-Spiced Pumpkin Muffins

Ingredients:

- 1 1/2 cups all-purpose flour
- 1 teaspoon baking powder
- 1/2 teaspoon baking soda
- 1/2 teaspoon salt
- 1 teaspoon ground cinnamon
- 1/2 teaspoon ground nutmeg
- 1/4 teaspoon ground cloves
- 1/2 cup granulated sugar
- 1/2 cup packed brown sugar
- 1/2 cup vegetable oil or melted coconut oil
- 1 cup canned pumpkin (not pumpkin pie filling)
- 2 large eggs
- 1/4 cup milk (dairy or non-dairy)
- 1 teaspoon vanilla extract
- Optional: 1/2 cup chopped nuts (such as walnuts or pecans) or chocolate chips

Instructions:

1. **Preheat the Oven:**
   - Preheat your oven to 350°F (175°C). Line a muffin tin with paper liners or lightly grease the muffin cups.
2. **Mix Dry Ingredients:**
   - In a medium bowl, whisk together the flour, baking powder, baking soda, salt, cinnamon, nutmeg, and cloves. Set aside.
3. **Combine Wet Ingredients:**
   - In a large bowl, beat together the granulated sugar, brown sugar, and oil until well combined. Add the pumpkin, eggs, milk, and vanilla extract, and mix until smooth.
4. **Combine Dry and Wet Ingredients:**
   - Gradually add the dry ingredients to the wet ingredients, stirring until just combined. Be careful not to overmix. If you're using nuts or chocolate chips, fold them in gently at this stage.
5. **Fill Muffin Cups:**
   - Divide the batter evenly among the muffin cups, filling each about 3/4 full.
6. **Bake:**
   - Bake in the preheated oven for 18-22 minutes, or until a toothpick inserted into the center of a muffin comes out clean. The tops should be golden brown.
7. **Cool:**
   - Allow the muffins to cool in the pan for about 5 minutes before transferring them to a wire rack to cool completely.

Tips:

- **Pumpkin Purée:** Use pure pumpkin purée for best results. Avoid pumpkin pie filling, which has added spices and sugar.

- **Texture:** For a lighter texture, you can sift the flour before measuring.
- **Storage:** Store muffins in an airtight container at room temperature for up to 3 days. They can also be frozen for up to 3 months. To freeze, place muffins in a zip-top bag or airtight container.

Cinnamon-Spiced Pumpkin Muffins are a delightful treat that captures the essence of autumn in every bite. Enjoy them with a cup of coffee or tea for a cozy and satisfying snack!

Cinnamon Orange Bread

Ingredients:

For the Bread:

- 1 1/2 cups all-purpose flour
- 1 cup granulated sugar
- 1 1/2 teaspoons baking powder
- 1/2 teaspoon baking soda
- 1/2 teaspoon salt
- 1 teaspoon ground cinnamon
- 1/2 cup unsalted butter, softened
- 2 large eggs
- 1/2 cup freshly squeezed orange juice
- 1 tablespoon orange zest (from about 1 orange)
- 1/2 teaspoon vanilla extract

For the Cinnamon Sugar Swirl:

- 1/4 cup granulated sugar
- 1 tablespoon ground cinnamon

For the Orange Glaze (Optional):

- 1 cup powdered sugar
- 2-3 tablespoons freshly squeezed orange juice
- 1/2 teaspoon orange zest

Instructions:

1. **Preheat the Oven:**
   - Preheat your oven to 350°F (175°C). Grease and flour a 9x5-inch loaf pan, or line it with parchment paper.
2. **Prepare the Cinnamon Sugar Swirl:**
   - In a small bowl, mix together the granulated sugar and ground cinnamon. Set aside.
3. **Mix Dry Ingredients:**
   - In a medium bowl, whisk together the flour, baking powder, baking soda, salt, and ground cinnamon.
4. **Cream Butter and Sugar:**
   - In a large bowl, beat the softened butter and granulated sugar together until light and fluffy.
5. **Add Eggs and Orange:**
   - Beat in the eggs one at a time, mixing well after each addition. Stir in the orange juice, orange zest, and vanilla extract.
6. **Combine Ingredients:**
   - Gradually add the dry ingredients to the wet ingredients, mixing until just combined. Be careful not to overmix.

7. **Layer and Swirl:**
   - Pour half of the batter into the prepared loaf pan. Sprinkle half of the cinnamon sugar mixture evenly over the batter. Pour the remaining batter on top and sprinkle with the remaining cinnamon sugar mixture. Use a knife or skewer to gently swirl the cinnamon sugar into the batter.
8. **Bake:**
   - Bake in the preheated oven for 50-60 minutes, or until a toothpick inserted into the center of the bread comes out clean. The top should be golden brown.
9. **Cool:**
   - Allow the bread to cool in the pan for about 10 minutes before transferring it to a wire rack to cool completely.
10. **Prepare the Glaze (Optional):**
    - In a small bowl, whisk together the powdered sugar, orange juice, and orange zest until smooth. Drizzle over the cooled bread if desired.

Tips:

- **Orange Zest:** For a more intense orange flavor, you can increase the amount of orange zest.
- **Swirling:** Be gentle when swirling the cinnamon sugar to avoid overmixing and to create a nice swirl effect.
- **Storage:** Store the bread in an airtight container at room temperature for up to 3 days. It can also be frozen for up to 3 months. To freeze, wrap tightly in plastic wrap and foil.

Cinnamon Orange Bread is a delightful treat that combines sweet and spicy flavors with a refreshing citrus twist. Enjoy it on its own or with a cup of tea or coffee!

Cinnamon Rice Cakes

Ingredients:

- 4 cups rice cakes (plain or lightly salted)
- 1/4 cup granulated sugar
- 1 tablespoon ground cinnamon
- 2 tablespoons unsalted butter, melted (or use coconut oil for a dairy-free option)

Optional Toppings:

- Fresh fruit (e.g., apple slices, berries)
- Nut butter (e.g., almond butter, peanut butter)
- Yogurt

Instructions:

1. **Prepare the Cinnamon Sugar:**
   - In a small bowl, mix together the granulated sugar and ground cinnamon until well combined.
2. **Brush the Rice Cakes:**
   - Brush the rice cakes lightly with melted butter or coconut oil. This will help the cinnamon sugar adhere to the rice cakes and add flavor.
3. **Coat with Cinnamon Sugar:**
   - Sprinkle the cinnamon sugar mixture evenly over the buttered rice cakes. You can use a spoon or a small sieve to ensure an even coating.
4. **Serve:**
   - Enjoy the cinnamon rice cakes as they are, or add optional toppings like fresh fruit, nut butter, or yogurt for added flavor and nutrition.

Tips:

- **Rice Cake Variety:** You can use any type of rice cakes, including plain or lightly salted. If you prefer a less sweet version, use less sugar or omit it altogether.
- **Butter Alternatives:** For a dairy-free option, use melted coconut oil or a plant-based butter substitute.
- **Storage:** Cinnamon rice cakes are best enjoyed fresh, but you can store them in an airtight container at room temperature for up to a week. The coating may soften over time, so they are best eaten shortly after preparation.

Cinnamon Rice Cakes are a quick and easy snack that delivers a satisfying crunch and a burst of cinnamon sweetness. Enjoy them on their own or with your favorite toppings!

Cinnamon-Spiced Hot Cider

Ingredients:

- 4 cups apple cider (or apple juice if cider is not available)
- 2 cinnamon sticks
- 4-6 whole cloves
- 1/4 teaspoon ground nutmeg
- 1/4 cup brown sugar (optional, for extra sweetness)
- 1 orange, sliced (optional, for garnish)
- 1 apple, sliced (optional, for garnish)

Instructions:

1. **Combine Ingredients:**
    - In a large pot, combine the apple cider, cinnamon sticks, cloves, and ground nutmeg. If you're adding brown sugar for extra sweetness, stir it in at this stage.
2. **Heat the Cider:**
    - Bring the mixture to a gentle simmer over medium heat. Once it starts to simmer, reduce the heat to low and let it cook for 10-15 minutes, allowing the spices to infuse into the cider. Stir occasionally.
3. **Strain the Cider:**
    - After the cider has been spiced to your liking, remove it from the heat. Strain the cider through a fine-mesh strainer to remove the cinnamon sticks, cloves, and any other solids.
4. **Serve:**
    - Pour the hot cider into mugs. Garnish with fresh orange slices and apple slices if desired. You can also add an extra cinnamon stick to each mug for an additional touch of flavor.
5. **Enjoy:**
    - Serve the hot cider immediately while it's still warm. It's perfect on its own or accompanied by cookies or pastries.

Tips:

- **Sweetness:** Adjust the sweetness to your taste. If the cider is too tart, add more brown sugar or honey to sweeten it.
- **Spices:** Feel free to adjust the amount of spices based on your preference. You can add a pinch of ground ginger for an extra kick.
- **Make Ahead:** You can prepare the cider ahead of time and keep it warm in a slow cooker or thermos. Just be sure to strain it before serving.

Cinnamon-Spiced Hot Cider is a festive and warming drink that's perfect for autumn and winter gatherings. Enjoy the comforting aroma and rich flavor of this seasonal favorite!

Cinnamon Banana Smoothie

Ingredients:

- 2 ripe bananas
- 1 cup milk (dairy or non-dairy, such as almond, soy, or oat milk)
- 1/2 cup Greek yogurt (plain or vanilla; optional for added creaminess)
- 1 tablespoon honey or maple syrup (optional, for sweetness)
- 1/2 teaspoon ground cinnamon
- 1/4 teaspoon vanilla extract (optional)
- Ice cubes (optional, for a thicker texture)
- A pinch of salt (optional)

Instructions:

1. **Prepare the Ingredients:**
   - Peel and slice the bananas. If you prefer a colder, thicker smoothie, you can freeze the banana slices ahead of time.
2. **Blend the Smoothie:**
   - In a blender, combine the banana slices, milk, Greek yogurt (if using), honey or maple syrup (if using), ground cinnamon, and vanilla extract (if using). Add a pinch of salt if desired.
3. **Blend Until Smooth:**
   - Blend on high speed until the mixture is smooth and creamy. If you prefer a thicker smoothie, add a few ice cubes and blend again until smooth.
4. **Taste and Adjust:**
   - Taste the smoothie and adjust the sweetness or cinnamon if needed. You can add more honey, maple syrup, or cinnamon to suit your preference.
5. **Serve:**
   - Pour the smoothie into glasses and serve immediately.

Tips:

- **Frozen Bananas:** Using frozen bananas will give your smoothie a thicker, creamier texture and keep it cool without needing extra ice.
- **Protein Boost:** For an extra protein boost, consider adding a scoop of protein powder or a tablespoon of chia seeds.
- **Spice Variations:** Experiment with other spices like nutmeg or ginger for a different flavor twist.

Cinnamon Banana Smoothie is a flavorful and nutritious option that's easy to make and enjoyable any time of the day. Enjoy its creamy texture and warm cinnamon flavor!

Cinnamon Roll Bars

Ingredients:

For the Bars:

- 2 1/2 cups all-purpose flour
- 1/2 cup granulated sugar
- 1 tablespoon baking powder
- 1/2 teaspoon salt
- 1/2 cup unsalted butter, cold and cut into small pieces
- 1 cup milk (dairy or non-dairy)
- 1 large egg
- 1 teaspoon vanilla extract

For the Cinnamon Swirl:

- 1/2 cup packed brown sugar
- 2 tablespoons ground cinnamon
- 2 tablespoons unsalted butter, melted

For the Cream Cheese Glaze (Optional):

- 2 ounces cream cheese, softened
- 1 cup powdered sugar
- 1/4 cup milk (more if needed)
- 1/2 teaspoon vanilla extract

Instructions:

1. **Preheat the Oven:**
   - Preheat your oven to 350°F (175°C). Grease and flour a 9x13-inch baking pan or line it with parchment paper.
2. **Prepare the Cinnamon Swirl:**
   - In a small bowl, mix together the brown sugar, ground cinnamon, and melted butter until well combined. Set aside.
3. **Mix Dry Ingredients:**
   - In a large bowl, whisk together the flour, granulated sugar, baking powder, and salt.
4. **Cut in the Butter:**
   - Add the cold, cut-up butter to the dry ingredients. Use a pastry cutter or your fingers to work the butter into the flour mixture until it resembles coarse crumbs.
5. **Add Wet Ingredients:**
   - In a separate bowl, whisk together the milk, egg, and vanilla extract. Add this mixture to the flour mixture and stir until just combined. Do not overmix.
6. **Assemble the Bars:**
   - Spread half of the batter evenly in the prepared baking pan. Sprinkle the cinnamon swirl mixture evenly over the batter. Drop spoonfuls of the remaining

batter on top of the cinnamon mixture and gently spread to cover. Swirl the batter with a knife or skewer to create a marbled effect.
7. **Bake:**
   - Bake in the preheated oven for 30-35 minutes, or until a toothpick inserted into the center comes out clean. The top should be golden brown.
8. **Prepare the Cream Cheese Glaze (Optional):**
   - While the bars are cooling, prepare the glaze. In a medium bowl, beat the softened cream cheese until smooth. Gradually add the powdered sugar and milk, mixing until you reach your desired consistency. Stir in the vanilla extract.
9. **Glaze and Serve:**
   - Once the bars are completely cool, spread the cream cheese glaze over the top. Cut into squares and serve.

Tips:

- **Swirling:** To achieve a good swirl effect, don't overmix the batter. A gentle swirl will create a nice marbled appearance.
- **Texture:** These bars are best enjoyed fresh but can be stored in an airtight container at room temperature for up to 3 days. They can also be frozen for up to 3 months.
- **Variations:** You can add chopped nuts or raisins to the cinnamon swirl for extra texture and flavor.

Cinnamon Roll Bars offer all the delicious flavors of cinnamon rolls in a simpler, easier-to-make form. Enjoy these sweet, gooey treats with a cup of coffee or tea!

Cinnamon Apple Stuffed Pancakes

Ingredients:

For the Apple Filling:

- 2 medium apples, peeled, cored, and diced
- 2 tablespoons unsalted butter
- 1/4 cup granulated sugar
- 1 teaspoon ground cinnamon
- 1/4 teaspoon ground nutmeg
- 1 tablespoon all-purpose flour (optional, for thickening)

For the Pancakes:

- 1 1/2 cups all-purpose flour
- 2 tablespoons granulated sugar
- 1 tablespoon baking powder
- 1/2 teaspoon salt
- 1 cup milk (dairy or non-dairy)
- 1 large egg
- 2 tablespoons unsalted butter, melted
- 1 teaspoon vanilla extract

For Serving (Optional):

- Maple syrup
- Powdered sugar
- Whipped cream

Instructions:

1. **Prepare the Apple Filling:**
   - In a medium skillet, melt the butter over medium heat. Add the diced apples, granulated sugar, cinnamon, and nutmeg. Cook, stirring occasionally, until the apples are tender and the mixture is thickened, about 5-7 minutes. If the filling is too runny, stir in the flour and cook for another minute. Remove from heat and let cool slightly.
2. **Prepare the Pancake Batter:**
   - In a large bowl, whisk together the flour, sugar, baking powder, and salt. In a separate bowl, mix the milk, egg, melted butter, and vanilla extract. Pour the wet ingredients into the dry ingredients and stir until just combined. The batter will be lumpy, which is okay. Avoid overmixing.
3. **Cook the Pancakes:**
   - Heat a nonstick skillet or griddle over medium heat and lightly grease with butter or oil. For each pancake, pour about 1/4 cup of batter onto the skillet. Spread the batter slightly to form a small circle. Spoon a tablespoon of the apple filling onto

the center of the pancake. Top with a bit more pancake batter, covering the filling completely.
4. **Flip and Cook:**
    - Cook until bubbles form on the surface of the pancake and the edges look set, about 2-3 minutes. Carefully flip the pancake and cook for another 2-3 minutes, or until golden brown and cooked through. Repeat with the remaining batter and apple filling.
5. **Serve:**
    - Serve the cinnamon apple stuffed pancakes warm, drizzled with maple syrup and dusted with powdered sugar if desired. Add a dollop of whipped cream for extra indulgence.

Tips:

- **Apples:** Use firm apples like Granny Smith or Honeycrisp for the best texture and flavor.
- **Consistency:** Ensure the apple filling is thick enough so it doesn't leak out when cooking the pancakes.
- **Cooking:** Cook pancakes on medium heat to ensure they cook through without burning.

Cinnamon Apple Stuffed Pancakes combine the comforting flavors of apple pie with the fluffy goodness of pancakes, making for a delicious and satisfying breakfast or brunch treat. Enjoy!

www.ingramcontent.com/pod-product-compliance
Lightning Source LLC
LaVergne TN
LVHW081607060526
838201LV00054B/2121